# THE LAW OF INHERITANCE

# TO CHIEFSHIPS

## AS OBSERVED BY THE SIKHS

## PREVIOUS TO THE ANNEXATION

## OF THE PANJAB

# THE LAW OF INHERITANCE

# TO CHIEFSHIPS

## AS OBSERVED BY THE SIKHS

## PREVIOUS TO THE ANNEXATION

## OF THE PANJAB

BY

LEPEL GRIFFIN, B. C. S.

GYAN

*Published by*

GYAN

Gyan Publishing House
5, Ansari Road
Daryaganj, New Delhi-110002
Phone: 011-47034999, 9811692060
E-mail: books@gyanbooks.com

*Distribution Network*
gyanbooks.com
India, USA, Canada, UK, Australia



ISBN: 978-93-6208-363-0 (PB)
First Published, 1869

2nd Impression 2024

*Printed at:* Gyan Press, Delhi.



**A LARGER GRAMMAR OF THE TAMIL LANGUAGE IN BOTH ITS DIALECTS**

Author: G. U. POPE

# THE LAW OF INHERITANCE

# TO CHIEFSHIPS

AS OBSERVED BY THE SIKHS

PREVIOUS TO THE ANNEXATION

OF THE PANJAB.

BY

LEPEL GRIFFIN, B. C. S.;

AUTHOR OF "THE PANJAB CHIEFS."

*LAHORE.*

*Punjab Printing Company, Limited.*

*1869.*

# PREFACE.

A treatise on the Law of Inheritance to Sikh chiefships, as in force, previous to the annexation of the Panjáb, possesses little more than a historical value. But it is difficult to understand the history of the Panjáb, or the growth of the Sikh power, Trans and Cis-Satlej, without a knowledge of the laws and customs which, even in the days of the greatest anarchy and violence, were acknowledged generally by the chiefs, and which, in the majority of cases, were observed by them. A long and uninterrupted peace, the declared wish of Government that the chiefships should be perpetuated, and the protection and security that all enjoy under British rule, has not been without its effect upon the Sikhs, who have abandoned or modified many of their peculiar customs, and have adopted a more uniform system of law. But it will not be the less interesting, to the historical student, to determine the customs observed by the founders of the Sikh power, which, even though they may have lost much of their original force and significance, nevertheless possess an influence which will be felt for many years to come.

The authorities for what has been advanced in this treatise are the family records of the chiefs concerned, and the statements of their confidential agents, the political records of the Dehli Residency and the Ambala Agency from the year 1808 ; and disputed cases decided by many political officers, including Sir David Ochterlony, Sir Charles Melcalfe, Captain Birch, Captain Murray, Sir George Clerk, Captain Ross, Captain Wade, Sir Henry Lawrence, and Major Broadfoot.

# INDEX.

## A.



## B.

C.

## D.



## E.



## F.



## G.



## H.

## I.



## J.



## K.



## L.

## M.



## N.



## P.

## W.

# THE LAW OF INHERITANCE

# TO CHIEFSHIPS

## AS OBSERVED BY THE SIKHS

### PREVIOUS TO THE ANNEXATION OF THE PANJAB.

1. It is necessary to consider the origin and development of the Sikh Chiefships, before the rules of succession, which obtain amongst them, can be accurately determined, for these have grown up gradually and without abruptness, and have been modified, as much by a remembrance of the Hindu Code, by which the Sikhs were bound before they adopted the reformed faith, as by the exercise of almost uncontrolled power, which, in a time of license and confusion, made the will of the strongest often the only law.

*The origin and growth of the Sikh Chiefships must be considered before their laws can be understood.*

2. To declare, authoritatively, the laws that prevailed among the Sikhs, is a matter of great difficulty, and one which has often been pronounced impossible. Principles were little re-

*The difficulty of ascertaining the Sikh law is very considerable.*

garded by them; prescription and custom, modified by various disturbing influences, were the only acknowledged guides; whilst there is no family of any importance which has not, when its interest has seemed to require it, denied or evaded the rules which it has ordinarily been content to follow. Yet it is possible, by a careful consideration of the precedents which Sikh history furnishes in abundance, to determine what were the general rules by which particular families, or the whole body of Sikh Chiefs, were commonly bound, and to declare, with tolerable certainty, the reasons which led to their disregard or denial, under exceptional circumstances.

*The two main divisions of the Sikhs: into those of the Mánjha and Málwa.*

3. The Sikhs have been divided into two great classes, named from the districts they inhabit, the Mánjha and the Málwa, and the origin and history of these are altogether different. The "Mánjha" is the name of the southern portion of the Bári Doáb, in the neighbourhood of the cities of Lahore and Amritsar; and the Mánjha Sikhs, by a convenient enlargement of the term, may be held to include all those who, at the time of the final dissolution of the Muhammadan power, were located to the north of the river Satlej. Málwa is the county immediately to the south of the same

river, stretching towards Dehli and Bikanír, and the Sikhs who inhabit this district, being the original settlers and not mere invaders or immigrants from the Mánjha, are known as the Málwa Sikhs. Their acknowledged head is the great Phúlkián house, of which the Maháraja of Pattiála is the representative, with the closely allied families of Nábha, Jhínd, Bhadour, Malod, Badrúka, Jiúndan, Diálpúra, Laudgharia, Rámpur and Kot Dhuna, and the more distantly connected houses of Farídkot and Kythal.

*The origin of the Málwa Sikhs.*

4. The ancestors of the Málwa chiefs were simple Hindu peasants, mostly of Rájpút extraction, who, about the middle of the sixteenth century, emigrated from the neighbourhood of Jassalmír. They were peaceful subjects of the Muhammadan rulers of Dehli, and strictly observed the Hindu Law with regard to succession to real and personal property as well as in all other particulars.

*They rise from mere peasants into the position of land-owners.*

5. In the course of a hundred years, in proportion as the central authority at Dehli grew weak, the power of the Jat settlers increased. They were *málguzárs*, or payers of revenue into the Imperial treasury, and made no effort to shake off a yoke which was in no way galling; but they acquired

large grants of land, founded villages, and became wealthy and of some social importance. They continued, moreover, like other Hindus, to follow the ordinances of Manu and the Shástras.

*They adopt Sikhism, and gradually become independent of the Muhammadan Government.*

6. But at the beginning of the eighteenth century, the Málwa chiefs abandoned Hinduism for the new faith which was then being preached by Govind, the last and the most influential of the Sikh Gúrús. The hundred years that followed was an era of anarchy. The great Muhammadan empire was, from inherent weakness, falling asunder, and the Sikhs, day by day, gained power and territory at the expense of their nominal masters, who persecuted the new faith but were unable to destroy it. Sikhism was then, as Muhammadanism in the seventh and eighth centuries, and Wahabeeism in the present, a religion of the sword, and the new converts appeared as ready to fight with each other as with the common enemy, against whom alone they ever united. The Sikhs did not avowedly abandon the Hindu Codes of Law, which they had, from time immemorial, obeyed; and neither Nának nor Govind had laid down new rules by which their followers should be bound in matters of succession and inheritance; but they felt a contempt for Hinduism, with its restric-

tions and prejudices, and refused to follow its precepts whenever these were opposed to their immediate interests. Society was in a state of disintegration and demoralization. Each man did what was right in his own eyes, and whatever he was able to do with impunity appeared to him right. Widows and orphans had no helper against the powerful neighbours who divided their lands amongst them at their pleasure; and the only means by which the smaller chiefs could escape absorption was by attaching themselves, as feudal retainers or vassals, to the great houses, who were able and willing to protect them in return for service in the field. Thus arose the great Cis-Satlej chiefs, whose obscure origin and unprincipled acquisitions were ennobled by titles extorted from the Emperor of Dehli, who was still the nominal ruler of the Málwa, and who was too weak and timid to refuse to honour the men whom he knew to be the most formidable enemies of his power.

*The reasons which led them to seek the protection of the British Government.*

7. At the beginning of the present century the fate which the Cis-Satlej chiefs had so often brought upon others seemed likely to become their own. Ranjít Singh, Maháraja of Lahore, having reduced to submission the chiefs in the neighbourhood of his capital, determined to conquer the

whole country to the south of the Satlej, as far as the river Jamna, which, he believed, he might safely accomplish without coming into collision with the English power. The condition of the Cis-Satlej States eminently favored the success of his design. Jealous of each other, and with no common bond of union, now that the Muhammadan power had finally collapsed, they would, one by one, have fallen victims to the energy and determination of Ranjít Singh, whose ambition knew no limits and no scruples, and to whom the very names of honour and pity were unknown. The Málwa chiefs saw their danger in time, and, at the very moment when their annihilation seemed inevitable, threw themselves on the mercy of the British Government, which, after much hesitation, accepted the position and declared the Cis-Satlej territory under its protection.

*The period of quiet during which Sikh laws became somewhat consolidated.*

8. Then followed a period of unbroken security, during which the strong power which prevented any attack from without, insisted upon tranquility within, and maintained the smallest as well as the largest States in the possession of the dignity and power which they had possessed when first they claimed its protection. It was during this period that the rules of succession became, to a certain

degree, uniform and consistent, although it will be understood that these are but comparative terms when applied to laws that prevailed in a society so exceptionally constituted, which had learned so lately the advantages of order, and which had been accustomed for so long to consider license synonymous with liberty.

*The war of 1845 made great changes in the relations of the British Government with the Cis-Satlej States.*

9. The effect of the Satlej campaign of 1845-46 was almost precisely similar to that caused by the campaign of 1866 in Northern Germany. The British Government, which had, for years, deplored a state of things which it was unable, without breaking faith with the chiefs, to rectify; which had seen the people oppressed and ground down by petty tyrants, who possessed absolute power in their respective States, seized the opportunity which the folly and ingratitude of the chiefs had given, to inaugurate a new order of things. The most important chiefs alone were permitted to retain their power, while that of the smaller ones was taken altogether away: they were declared mere *Jagírdárs* of the British Government, and the whole of their territories was placed under the control of British Officers and British Courts of Law.

*The Málwa chiefships have gradually developed.*

10. It will thus appear that the Málwa chiefs have passed through several distinct periods of development. First, the mere cultivators of the lands on which, as immigrants, they had settled; then, the owners of those same lands. Next came the period of conflict with the Muhammadan power, during which the chiefships grew up gradually and naturally, followed by the period of tranquillity which was the consequence of their claiming British protection. The last period saw the majority of them stripped of the power which they had infamously abused, and which it was a misfortune to the country that they ever had possessed.

*The Sikh chiefs of the Mánjha had an origin very different from that of the Málwa chiefs.*

11. There is no gradual development such as this to be traced in the history of the Sikh chiefs of the Mánjha. Scarcely more than a hundred years ago, the majority of them were cultivators of the soil, enjoying none of the consideration which the Cis-Satlej chiefs had, for long, received from the Court of Dehli. With the last invasions of Ahmad Sháh and the Afgháns, they rose to sudden power, and every man who had energy and courage gathered a band of marauders about him and plundered the country, seizing and holding whatever lands he could. Many of these Sikhs crossed the Satlej and ravaged the country to the very gates of

Dehli; while some of them seized large tracts of land Cis-Satlej, which they continued to hold against all comers, by the sword alone, a tenure altogether different from that of their Málwa neighbours, and more resembling that of a Norman baron settled in the Welsh Marches, seven hundred years ago.

*The rise of Mahárája Ranjít Singh to power, and its effects.*

The ascendancy of the Sikhs in the Panjab Trans-Satlej, was but brief. Mahárája Ranjít Singh subdued them one by one; Rámgharias, Bhangis, Kanheyas, all the great houses fell in turn, and so completely, that the chiefships became merely nominal, dependent on the will of the Sovereign of Lahore; while the laws of succession were practically swept away before they had time to crystallize into their natural form. It will thus be readily perceived that it is in the Cis-Satlej States alone that a search for precedents, which may throw some real light on Sikh practice, is likely to be successful. One great Trans-Satlej chief alone, Sirdar Fatah Singh, Ahluwália, the grandfather of the present Rája of Kapúrthalla, held his own against the ambition of the ruler of Lahore; but he had large Cis-Satlej possessions, which were under British protection, and he held up the name of England as a shield against the Mahárája successfully, though it is certain that the British Government would not have interfered to save his estates in the Jalandhar Doáb, with which they had no possible interest. This Sirdár, then, must be considered as a Cis-Satlej chief, and his family has commonly followed the usages of the Málwa Sikhs.

*Primogeniture only observed in the principal Phúlkián families.*

12. The ordinary rule of succession to Sikh chiefships was equal division among the sons, and primogeniture has only prevailed in the three principal branches of the Phúlkián family, namely, Pattiála, Nábha and Jhínd, and perhaps in the connected house of Farídkot. The declarations of the chiefs themselves can be depended upon but little, for they have asserted different principles at different times, to serve their immediate interests. In the course of the dispute regarding the succession to the Jhínd State, in 1836, the agents of Pattiála, Kythal, Nábha and Bazídpúr declared—

*The chiefs declare that primogeniture is the rule of the Phúlkián and Bháikián families.*

"It would seem that Jhínd has been taken possession of by the "British Government in consequence of the descendants of Bhúp Singh "having received a separate maintenance, and having long lived apart "from the elder branch of the family, but there is nothing unusual in "such a circumstance, but, on the contrary, it is in exact conformity "with the uniform practice of the houses Phúlkián and Bháikián, in "which the eldest son always succeeds to the whole estate, with the "exception of small portions set apart for the maintenance of younger "children."

*They, nevertheless, twenty years before, declared the rule was equal partition among*

13. The Phúlkián family, however, consists, as has before been shown, of eleven houses, and

in a dispute which, in 1816, had arisen between two of them, namely Badrúka and Bazídpúr, the very chiefs who, in 1836, declared that primogeniture was the universal rule, wrote to Sir David Ochterlony that the customs of the smaller Phúlkián houses prescribed an equal partition of inheritance among the sons.

*the sons.*

*In the dispute between the Rájá of Pattiála and his brother, they assert both positions alternately.*

A third case yet more strongly shows how little weight can be placed on the formal declarations of the chiefs. On the death of Raja Sáhib Singh of Pattiála, his second son, Ajít Singh, advanced a claim to half the territory. This claim was submitted to the different Phúlkián chiefs for their opinion. They declared Ajít Singh entitled to an equal share of all the ancestral estates of his father, in accordance with the custom of the protected Sikh States generally, and the Phúlkián houses in particular. Yet, subsequently, swayed by other motives, several of the chiefs addressed the resident at Dehli to the effect that their former statement was only given at the request of Sirdár Ajít Singh, and that the true rule of succession among them was that the whole estate devolved on the eldest son, subject to a provision for the younger sons.

The truth lay between these conflicting statements, nor have the Phúlkián or Bháikián chiefs ever adhered uniformly to one rule or the other, and the disputed cases which were referred to them were decided by no fixed law. Yet it is evident that primogeniture has prevailed only in the three families of Pattiála, Nábha and Jhínd, and all the others have adopted the custom of equal partition among sons, with the exception of those cases in which Pattiála, arbitrarily, and for reasons of its own, has awarded a larger share to the eldest, the second or even the youngest son. Under the influence of this rule of equal partition the Bhadour estate has been broken up into several chiefships, that of Malod into two, and in the same way with other families. Even in these three exceptional cases the deviation has only taken place within the last hundred years, and contrary to what they, with the exception of Pattiála, declared, so lately as 1836, to be their own law of inheritance (1). And although Pattiála, Nábha and Jhínd have adhered to the rule of primogeniture, yet even these have made attempts to set it aside, as, in 1812, when Rája Bhág Singh of Jhínd desired his second son Partáb Singh to succeed him, and delivered a paper to that effect to Sir D. Ochterlony, which

(1) Letter of Mr. Clerk, 30th November 1836, to Mr. T. Metcalfe.

the British Government declined to sanction.

14. There are numerous precedents in the Phúlkián families which will support the above position, *Precedents from Phúlkián families showing that primogeniture was not the rule amongst them.*

(*a.*) Sirdárs Díp Singh and Bír Singh divided the estate between them. *The State of Bhadour.*

(*b.*) On the death of Sirdar Bír Singh, his three sons, Jowáhir Singh, Jaimal Singh and Jaggat Singh, divided his possessions equally, except that the eldest received a somewhat larger share (*Sirdari kharach*) as the representative of the family, and on the death of Jowáhir Singh, without male issue, his estate was assigned, by Pattiála, to Khazán Singh, the son of the second brother.

(*c.*) Sirdar Mohr Singh of Bhadour had three sons, Amrik Singh, Samand Singh and Suján Singh. On his death, the estate was divided between them equally, except that Samand Singh, the *second* son, received a somewhat larger share than his brother.

(*d.*) Sirdar Mán Singh had two sons, Dalel Singh and Bágh Singh. On his death, the elder brother took two-thirds of the estate, and the *The State of Malod.*

younger, one-third.

(*e.*) On the death of Sirdar Dalel Singh, his two sons, Fatah Singh and Mith Singh, divided the estate in the same proportion. This decision was given by Pattiála, and pleased neither party, but they afterwards agreed to it; and the sons of Fatah Singh and Mith Singh followed the same rule, as did Bágh Singh, their uncle, so that the Malod custom may be affirmed to be that, of two sons, the elder takes two-thirds and the younger one-third of the estate.

*The State of Badrúka.*

(*f.*) In 1815, a dispute arose between the two Badrúka Sirdars, Karam Singh and Basáwa Singh, as to their respective shares, and the former, with the Pattiála Raja, addressed General Ochterlony to the effect that the smaller Phúlkián families inherited equally. The two Sirdárs accordingly divided the territory between them in equal shares.

(*g.*) Súkha Singh and Bhagwán Singh, the sons of Basáwa Singh, divided the estate equally between them.

*Precedents in the Bhaikián family showing that the rule of primogeniture which they profess was not observed by them.*

15. The Bhaikián families, although they protested that their rule was primogeniture, could not prove it to have been so. The fact was pre-

cisely the reverse. Gúrbaksh Singh, the head of the Bhai family of Kythal, died in 1765, leaving five sons, Búdh Singh, Desú Singh, Takht Singh, Dhanna Singh and Sukha Singh, among whom his estate was equally divided. Desú Singh became the most powerful, but this was only by his own conquests. His son Buhál Singh succeeded, not as the eldest, but because his brother Lál Singh, who had rebelled against his father, was in confinement at the time of Desú Singh's death. Lál Singh, however, escaped, defeated and murdered his brother, and seized the whole estate. This was the first occasion on which the chiefship and estates of Kythal went to one son, and it was by force of arms and not by custom. The rule of primogeniture was, after this, naturally asserted by Bhai Lál Singh, to cover his own illegal seizure of the estate. In the same manner, on the death of Bhai Bassáwa Singh, first cousin of Bhai Lál Singh, his territory was equally divided between his sons, Panjáb Singh, Guláb Singh and Sangat Singh.

*Precedents among other Sikh chiefships proving that primogeniture was not the Sikh rule, but partition, more or less equal, among the sons.*

16. The Phúlkián and Bhaikián houses are the only ones which have even pretended to follow the rule of primogeniture universally, and it has been shown that this pretence is contradicted by the facts. With regard to other chiefships Cis and

Trans-Satlej, the rule of equal partition was general, although where one son was the favorite of his father he might receive a larger share of the estate, and this, irrespective of his being the elder or younger; other cases there were in which the brothers quarreled, and each seized whatever share he could of his father's estate, in defiance of all laws of succession. This was not uncommon in early Sikh days, but not so common as to make the law of succession doubtful. The elder son moreover generally received a somewhat larger portion known as *Karach Sirdári*, as being the representative of the family, and to maintain the chiefship, but the division was practically equal.

(*a.*) *Sháhabád.*—On the death of Sirdár Karam Singh, his four sons, Ranjít Singh, Kharak Singh, Sher Singh and Káhn Singh divided the property.

(*b.*) *Kapúrthalla.*—Rája Nihál Singh desired to leave his principality to his youngest son Suchet Singh, and it was only the remonstrance of the British authorities which caused him to abandon the design. He then, by will, divided the estate among his sons, giving a larger share to the eldest.

(c). *Siálba.*—Sirdár Hari Singh divided his estate between his two sons, giving a larger share to the *younger*.

(d.), *Sindhánwália.*—On the death of Sirdár Didár Singh, his sons Gúrbuksh Singh, Amír Singh and Ruttan Singh succeeded equally.

(e.) *Attari.*—Sirdár Jodh Singh left two sons, Partáb Singh and Chattar Singh, who succeeded equally to the estate.

(f.) In the same family the three Sirdárs now living at Attari, Jiún Singh, Hari Singh and Ajít Singh hold the jagir of Shaikoran, in equal shares, and it will so descend to their heirs.

(g.) *Bhangi.*—Sirdar Gújar Singh, the head of the Bhangi confederacy, and an independent chief, divided his possessions between his two elder sons Súkha Singh and Sáhib Singh.

(h.) *Thanesar.*—This estate, on the death of Sirdar Mit Singh, was divided between his two nephews Bhág Singh and Bhanga Singh, in what is termed the *Panjtu* proportion ;—Bhanga Singh, although the younger, receiving 3-5*ths*, and Bhág Singh, the elder, 2-5*ths* only.

*The succession of the widow, failure of male issue.*

17. On failure of male heirs, the estate, according to ordinary Sikh law, descends to the widow for her life. This rule, which is asserted by all the principal families, with the exception of the Bhaikián and the Singhpúrias, is very much modified in practice. It will readily be understood that at a time when possessions which had been won by the sword had to be held by the sword, the succession of a woman, with the customary attendants of anarchy, favoritism and weakness, which left the State a prey to its powerful neighbours, was viewed with dislike and suspicion. Sikh women have shown themselves often capable of ruling with vigour and ability, and such examples as Ráni Aus Kour of Pattiála, Ráni Dya Kour of Ambálla, and Mai Sadda Kour, for long the acknowledged head of the great Kanheya confederacy, will always be remembered by the people with respect; but as a rule they were only distinguished from the women of the rest of India by a looser morality, and their succession to a chiefship was usually the precursor of its ruin. To obviate such a calamity Sikh custom asserted the right of the brother of the deceased to marry his widow, and thus to succeed, through the woman, to the estate. The right lay with the elder brother

*The custom of chaddarddína or karewa.*

but the widow was often allowed to make her choice, which naturally often fell on the younger brother of her husband. This form of marriage was known as *karewa* (*karí húí*, a woman who has been married), or *chaddardálna*, ('throwing a sheet'), from the chief ceremony observed. The '*karewa*' marriage was universally acknowledged as lawful, among the Jat Sikhs, and the issue as competent to succeed to landed and personal property; but it has never been considered of equal sanctity and authority with the regular marriage '*ryah*' or '*shàdi*,' which is contracted with a virgin; although the issue of the latter would, ordinarily, in case of dispute as to succession, be considered to have an equal claim, though this was sometimes denied, and the children of the regular *vyah* took precedence of the issue of the *karewa*. The families of Pattiála, Nábha and Jhínd have, of late years, agreed to abandon this custom altogether, it being now unnecessary, as the succession has been declared by Government to remain always with male heirs; but, as will hereafter be shown, they have frequently observed it in former years.

The *karewa* marriage is strictly that performed with a brother's widow only, and although it is also known as *chaddardálna*, yet this term is of a more extended meaning, and includes an informal marriage with women other than the brother's widow.

Among the Sikhs the first wife would often be married with the orthodox ceremonies, and wives married subsequently by the simpler ceremony, which, in many cases, was little more than an excuse for concubinage, nor were such wives considered as the equals of the one first married. If the women so married were of the same caste or tribe as the husband, and with whom he could lawfully have contracted a regular '*vyah*,' the issue was legitimate and competent to succeed; but if, as was often the case, they were of a different caste or *got* ( clan ), the issue was not considered as equal that of the *vyah*, and the wife was never permitted to eat with the wives of the husband's caste (*got kundla*). The informality of the custom caused it justly to be viewed with suspicion, and there have been many cases in Sikh families of women, who were no more than ordinary concubines, claiming, on the death of their lord, the estate for themselves or their sons, as lawful wives married by *chaddardálna*.

*seniority of* With regard to the seniority of widows, and

the marriage of sons, the opinion of all the chief Sikh families Cis-Satlej is unanimous.(1) The Pandits to whom the question was referred, declared the law to be that of the Mitakshara, which, in a house where there are many wives, asserts her to have seniority who is of the same caste as the husband. But this point of caste the Sikhs do not much regard, and she is the eldest wife to whom the chief was first married, a wife married by *shádi* ranking before her taken by *chaddar-dálna*.

*widows and the marriage of sons.*

The elder son loses his position should he be—married subsequently to his younger brother. The unanimous opinion of the chiefs above referred to was as follows:—

"If there be two uterine brothers betrothed in two families, and if "from any cause the marriage of the elder brother cannot take place, "and the parents of the girl to whom the younger brother is betrothed "be importunate for the marriage, the father will not permit his younger "son to be first married, because the performance to his forefathers of "the funeral rites &c., from the hands of an elder son could not take "place unless he had been married prior to his younger brother. The "marriage of the elder must, therefore, precede. If the younger son, "from the importunity of the girl's parents, be first married, and his "elder brother afterwards, then the performance of the funeral obsequies "to his forefathers are prohibited to him, and it may be said the younger "takes the place of the elder by reason of his being first married."

(1.) Pattiála, Jhínd, Khytal, Nábha, Thanesar, Bassi, Búria, Bhurtghar, Chichirowli, Shábabád, Jagadri, Buria and Gadowli,—*Vide* their replies of 10th January 1828; also those of Pandits Dias Raj, Chandar Máu and Misr Rikhi Kais of Pattiála, of the same date.

*Chundaband and Bhaiband the two ordinary modes of partition.*

The seniority of the wives does not however affect the succession of the sons. It has been shown that a preference is sometimes given to the children of an orthodox over the issue of an irregular or *chaddardálna* marriage, but in other cases the sons share equally.

Two methods of division, however, prevail among families in which the right of primogeniture is denied, known as *chundaband* and *bhaiband.* According to the first named, the estate is divided equally between the mothers, for their respective issue; and, in the second, it is divided equally among all the sons. Supposing a man to have left two wives, the elder having one son and the second three; by *chundàband* division the one son of the first wife would take half the estate, and the three sons of the second would divide the other half between them: by *bhaiband* division, all four sons would share equally. The custom of *chundaband* was almost entirely confined to the Sikhs of the Mánjha, while in the Málwa equal division was the rule.

*Precedents showing the custom of chaddardálna or karewa in the chief families.*

18. The following are cases which prove the existence of the custom of *chadda rdálna*, or *karewa*

and its legal value, in many of the principal Sikh families.

(*a.*) *Pattiála.* Raja Amar Singh married, by *chaddardálna*, the widow of his brother Himmat Singh, who died without male issue, and succeeded to the whole estate.

(*b.*) *Nábha.* Hamír Singh married, in the same manner, the widow of his brother Kappúr Singh, who died without issue, and succeeded to the estate. Raja Jaswant Singh was the issue of this marriage.

(*c.*) *Jhínd.* Sirdár Gajpat Singh married, by *chaddardálna*, the widow of his brother, Alam Singh, who died without male issue.

(*d.*) *Thanesar.*—Indar Sen married a woman named Hurruh, by whom he had a son Nodh Singh, who adopted the Sikh faith. On the death of Indar Sen, his brother Chandar Sen married the widow by *chaddardálna*, the issue being Bhág Singh and Bhanga Singh, the chiefs of Thanesar.

(*e.*) *Thanesar.* On the death of Sirdár Mehtáb Singh, his brother Guláb Singh married the widow and securod the estate.

(*f.*) *Shahíd.* Sirdárs Dharam Singh and Karam Singh were uterine brothers. On the death of the former, the latter married his two widows Hukma and Desa, by *karewa.* Hukma bore him two sons, Guláb Singh and Mehtáb Singh. The latter died, leaving two widows, Karam Kour and Sáhib Kour. The surviving brother Guláb Singh married Sáhib Kour by *karewa.*

(*g.*) *Rúpar.* Sirdár Hari Singh, a Mánjha Sikh, married one Rájan, *no connection of his own,* by *chaddardálna.* The two sons of this marriage, Sirdárs Dewa Singh and Charrat Singh, became, one, chief of Siálbah, and the other, chief of Rúpar.

(*h.*) *Lundhi.* Durgáha Singh was first married by *vyah* to Pardhoun. He then married, by *karewa,* Berin, the full sister of Pardhoun, who was a widow, and had been married to a distant relative of his own. The estate was divided among the sons of Pardhoun and Berin by *chundaband.*

(*i.*) *Mustaphabád.* Sirdárs Mehtáb Singh and Mirza Singh were uterine brothers. On the death of Mirza Singh his brother married the widow by *chaddardálna.*

(*j.*) *Kalsia.*—Sirdar Jodh Singh, Chief of Chichrouli, was the issue of a *chaddardálna* marriage contracted by Gúrbuksh Singh with a widow, of his tribe, but not previously connected with him. It is however also asserted that Jodh Singh was illegitimate, and that his mother was never married to Gúrbuksh Singh.

(*k.*) *Bhadour.*—Sirdár Kehr Singh married the widow of his brother Mehtáb Sing.

(*l.*) *Lashkar Khán.*—Sirdár Mohr Sing, head of the Nishánwála confederacy, married by *chaddardálna* the widow of his elder brother Anúp Singh, and obtained the chiefship and property.

(*m.*) *Ladwa.*—Sirdár Gúrdit Singh married the widow of his brother Sáhib Singh, and obtained the chiefship.

(*n.*) *Rangar Nangal.*—Sirdár Wazír Singh married, by *chaddardálna*, the widow of his brother Jamiyat Singh, who bore him Arjan Singh, and a daughter, who was married to Raja Dev-Indar Singh of Nábha, and became the mother of the present Rája.

All these precedents have been taken from *Among Sikhs of*

*Bráhman or Khatrí origin the custom of chaddardálna is not allowed, nor are the issue of such a marriage competent to inherit.*

the families of Jat Sikhs, resident both in the Mánjha and Málwa. But to all Sikhs of Bráhman or Khatrí origin, the re-marriage of widows, generally, and the marriage of a brother's widow in particular, is odious and unlawful, nor can the issue of such marriage legally inherit. Rája Tej Singh of Lahore, the Commander-in-Chief of the Sikh army, was a Gour Bràhman by birth, and adopted Sikhism in order to push his fortune more successfully at Lahore. In his old age he married the widow of his cousin Kishen Singh by what was called *chaddardálna*, and this lady some time after bore a son, Narindar Singh. The child is, however, incompetent to inherit: the issue of a chaddardálna marriage contracted by a Bráhman Sikh being illegitimate, and Harbans Singh, the brother of Tej Singh, and adopted by him before the birth of Narindar Singh, has inherited all the property. The Sikhs of Bràhman origin are few in number, but they maintain some of their Hindu prejudices and exclusiveness; although they are regarded as outcasts by orthodox Bràhmans, who will only give them their daughters in marriage for very large sums of money, and even then the girls are considered as dead, and have no further communication with their own family.

This is certainly the practice among Gour, Kanoujha, Sarrarieh and Dubbeh Bráhmans. The Sársút Bráhmans, who are the most numerous in the Panjab, are more liberal, and do not refuse intercourse with one of their number who has become a Sikh. Even among the stricter classes the son of a Bráhman Sikh may recover the position forfeited by his father, as Rája Harbans Singh has done. He has not taken the '*páhal*' the Sikh baptism, and follows the ordinary Bráhminical customs. That the feeling of caste superiority is not altogether lost when a Bráhman voluntarily abandons his caste, is shown by the refusal of Sirdar Bhúp Singh of Rúpar to betroth his daughter by a Bráhmani woman whom he had married by *chaddardálna*, to Dalíp Singh, Maharája of Lahore.

The priestly family of Bedis are Khatris. *The Khatri Sikhs.* Bishan Singh, the son of the famous Bedi Sáhib Singh, married by *chaddardálna* a widow of a family not related to him, and had issue Attar Singh, the father of Bábás Khem Singh and Sanpúran Singh. These last, though men of great influence among the Sikhs, are still considered as illegitimate, their father being the issue of a *chaddardálna* marriage, and cannot marry into families far their inferior in rank and influence.

Attar Singh inherited a mere fraction of the large estates owned by his father, and his sons Khem Singh and Sanpúran Singh lost even this; although, during the regency, they received small grants from the ancestral jagírs at Shàhpúr and Nasírpúr.

Other Khatri Sikh families are those of which Sirdars Jowàhir Singh Nalwa and Jhanda Singh Botàlia are the respective heads, but in neither of these had there been an instance of a *chaddardálna* marriage.

*Precedents regarding the right of widows to inherit in the Bhaikián and Singhpúria families. They were generally excluded.*

19. The right of widows to inherit was denied by the Bhaikiàn family of Khytal, and by the Singhpúria Sikhs. The latter, however much they may have denied the right, practically admitted it by allowing the custom of *chaddardálna* marriage to be observed in their family. Sirdàrs Búdh Singh and Súdh Singh Singhpúria were full brothers. On the death of the latter, Búdh Singh married his two widows, Sada Kour and Sukh Devi, and by these ladies he had six sons, who inherited two-thirds of the estate by *chundaband*, the other third being inherited by Amar Singh, born by a former regular marriage, thus proving that the issue of a *karewa* marriage was entitled to share equally with those of the

more orthodox *vyah*.

*Chadardálna not observed among the Bhaikiáns.*

The Bhaikiáns, however, did not permit the custom of *chaddardálna*, but the absolute denial of the right of the widow cannot be maintained in the presence of existing facts.

The general rule was certainly against the widow, as the following precedents will show.

(*a.*) Bhai Gúrdit Singh died without male issue, but leaving a widow; his two brothers, Lál Singh and Bassàwa Singh, divided the estate between them.

(*b.*) Bhai Charrat Singh died without male issue. His widow only received maintenance from Bhai Karam Singh, the brother, who inherited the estate.

(*c.*) Bhai Bahál Singh died without male issue, and Lál Singh, his younger brother, took the estate, giving a village to each of the widows.

(*d.*) Bhai Búdha Singh died without male issue, leaving four brothers, Dhanna Singh, Desú Singh, Takht Singh and Sukha Singh. The three latter of these took the whole estate, to the exclusion of the widow.

*Precedents in favor of the widow's right to inherit in the Bhaikián family.*

20. In three cases at least, in the Bhaikián family, the right of the widow to inherit was distinctly allowed. The first was on the death of Bhai Takht Singh, one of the four sons of Bhai Gúrbaksh Singh, the real founder of the family. His widow, Mai Sukha, not without opposition, inherited the estate of her husband, and held it for three years, when Bhai Lál Singh, Gúrdit Singh, Basáwa Singh and Karm Singh attacked her possessions, and having bought over the *zamindárs*, divided the estate between them. The second case, of Ráni Rattan Kour, is of a similar character; for although, on the death of her husband, she held the property four or five years, she was then ejected by the brothers of her husband, who divided it between them. Both these cases show a right, at first allowed, but subsequently over-ridden by violence and fraud.

*The Kakrála case.*

21. The third case is especially valuable, as the discussion on its merits, in 1811 and 1812, by Sir David Ochterlony, when the claim of the widow was admitted, and in 1818, on her death, by Mr. C. T. Metcalfe, and Captain Birch, Assistant Resident at Karnál, throws considerable light on many obscure points of Sikh law.

*The death of Bhai Karam Sing.*

Bhai Karam Singh was the son of Dhana Singh, and succeeded to his estates. He died in 1810, leaving a widow, Mai Bhágbari, and three daughters, all married, but only one, the wife of Sirdár Hamír Singh of Mani Majra having children. Bhai Lál Singh, the first cousin of Karam Singh, and head of the Kythal family, immediately claimed the estate. Sir David Ochterlony endeavoured at first to induce Lál Singh to relinquish his claim, or the widow to accept a compromise, but this, she, considering her right absolute and indefeasible, declined altogether to do. She was willing, however, to relinquish her claim in favor of Amar Singh, one of her grandsons by the wife of Sirdar Hamír Singh, and this Sir David was willing to recommend for sanction.

*The conflicting opinions of the chiefs.*

The Phúlkián Rájas at first declared in favor of the widow, but, subsequently, at the instigation of Bhai Lál Singh, asserted, in a document which Sir David Ochterlony stigmatized as framed, in his judgment, for the purpose of fraud, injustice and deception, that the widow had no right to inherit. That the chiefs asserted whatever was their interest or policy, without any regard to truth, is evident from numerous disputed cases in the first half of the present century, and as to Bhai Lál

Singh's denial of the right of the widow, it is notorious that he did oppose, and, by his influence and power, prevent Bassáwa Singh, his first cousin, taking possession of Tunansu, the estate of his full brother Gúrdit Singh, on the plea that the right of succession lay with the widow, and that for a considerable time she did exercise real authority and actually enjoy the revenue of these lands, and, nominally, both, till the day of her death.

*The decision of Government.*

The British Government, in 1812, decided in favor of the widow Mai Bhágbari, and she held the whole estate until her death in April 1818. She left a will in favor of her grandsons, the children of the Rája of Mani Majra, of whom the younger was her favorite kinsman, and was generally understood to be her adopted son. Bhai Lál Singh of Khytal at once asserted the claims which had been denied in 1812, in favor of the widow, and this time with more success.

*The case re-opened in 1818.*

In deciding in favor of Mai Bhágbari, in 1812, the Government had declared that the future descent would be considered on the death of the Ráni, as circumstances might alter it. The claimants were (1)—Bhai Lál Singh, first cousin of Karam Singh, Mai Bhágbari's husband; (2) Sirdárs

Goverdhan Singh and Amar Singh, sons of the Rája of Mani Majra; (3) Ráni Rattan Kour; (4) Sirdár Guláb Singh of Thanosar; and (5) Bhai Bassáwa Singh; and these claims it will be convenient to consider separately.

22. Bhai Lál Singh brought forward the same arguments which he had before used, that females were excluded from succession according to the custom of the Bhaikián house. This has been shown to be untrue, and force not custom had alone prevented women from obtaining what was generally acknowledged to be their rights. A declaration of Gúrú Rám Dás to the effect that the Bhaikiáns should adhere to the Khatri rule of inheritance and exclude women, was an invention easy to make, and, of course, difficult to disprove, were it not that Bhai Lál Singh himself had allowed on a former occasion the right of women to inherit.

*The several claims.*

*Bhai Lál Singh.*

(2.) Goverdhan Singh and Amar Singh, the sons of the Rája of Mani Majra, claimed, through their mother Ráni Chand Kour, the youngest daughter of Ráni Bhágbari, and produced, in support, a will said to have been executed in their favor, but to which there were no witnesses except her own officials, it being stated that no chief liked

*The Mani Majra Sirdárs.*

to affix his signature to the document and thus incur the wrath of the powerful Lál Singh. It was, moreover, notorious that the Ráni had long wished to adopt Amar Singh, the younger of the Rája's sons. He was about eleven years old at the time of her death, and had generally lived with her at Kakrála, from which place his marriage had taken place with a girl of the Balchappar family. The question of the validity of wills and the power of the widow to adopt will hereafter be considered.

*Ráni Rattan Kour.*

(3.) Ráni Rattan Kour was the childless widow of Bhai Hardás Singh, son of Karam Singh and Ráni Bhágbari. She founded her claim on the fact that her husband would have succeeded as heir had he been living.

*The Thanesar Chief.*

(4.) Sirdar Gulàb Singh of Thanesar claimed through his wife Sàhib Kour, the second daughter of Ràni Bhàgbari, who had borne him no children. The eldest daughter, Rattan Kour, he truly stated, had for long resided with her mother at Kakràla, and had a village assigned for her support.

*Bhai Basáwa Singh.*

(5.) The last claimant was Bhai Basàwa Singh, the first cousin of Bhai Làl Singh, with whom he claimed an equal share of the estate.

*The decision of Government.*

23. The Government might have treated the estate as an escheat without any impropriety. No one of the claims was good in law. Bhai Làl Singh, as a collateral, was not entitled to succeed. The Mani Majra chiefs were sons of a daughter, though whom the right to succession does not pass. Ràni Rattan Kour had no claim through her husband, he having died in the life-time of his father. Gulàb Singh of Thanesar claimed through his wife, who had no claim to succeed her mother: and Basàwa Singh was, as a collateral, in the same position as Làl Singh, and, moreover, he had signed a document by which he relinquished all claim to the Kakràla estate, in favor of Làl Singh. The Government had, however, no wish to take the estate, and in January 1819, the Governor General decided that—

"In order to preserve the territory of Kakrála undivided, as well "as to continue it in the family to which it has hitherto belonged, and "to prevent its being merged in the possessions of another family; "with a view also to obviate the difficulty of superseding the claim "of the elder married daughter of the late Karam Singh in favor of "the younger daughter or her children; the Governor General in Council "is pleased to resolve that the chiefship and territory of Kakrála shall "devolve on the representative heir of the late Bhai Lál Singh, the "existing head of the house of which Karam Singh was a member."

*A widow whose husband has died during the life-time of his father has no claim.*

24. The claim of Ràni Rattan Kour was not, as the preceding case has shown, allowed, and it may be considered as an invariable rule, against

which Rattan Kour could produce no precedent, that a widow whose husband has died during the life-time of his father has no claim whatever to inherit. One celebrated precedent did, however, exist, namely, Mai Sadda Kour Kanheya, whose case will be hereafter referred to, but which was of so exceptional a nature that it is valueless as proving or disproving a custom.

*The right of the widow constantly refused, and in practice she only succeeded when no brother or nephew of the husband existed.*

25. Although the right of the widow to inherit was generally admitted, and can even be proved to exist in families in which it was most pertinaciously denied, yet it is not to be supposed that, in rude times, when might was right, women were able to sustain their claims with any great success. To go beyond the Phúlkiàn family, to other Sikh houses in the Cis-Satlej States, it will be found that, in practice, in the generality of cases in which the widow succeeded, it was from failure of brothers or nephews of her husband, and that where they existed, they succeeded to the prejudice of the widow. The custom of *karewa* marriage, of course, chiefly accounts for this, the brother inheriting not from the deceased, but through the widow whom he married, and who had no power to prevent his thus obtaining possession of the property.

*Cases in which the right of the widow has been admitted, whether from failure of brothers or nephews or from her own superior right being allowed.*

*Lahore.*

(a.) On the death of Mahárája Kharak Singh of Lahore and his son Nao-Nihál Singh, the widow of the former, Ráni Chand Kour, was a claimant for the throne, and her right was admitted by a large and powerful party in the State, notwithstanding the existence of several reputed children of Mahárája Ranjít Singh. Prince Nao-Nihál Singh died the day after his father, previous to his installation as Mahárája, so that his widow Sàhib Kour was unable to put forward any personal claim, though her declaration that she was pregnant, at once invalidated the claim of Ráni Chand Kour to more than the regency, since, if a son were born to Ráni Sáhib Kour, he would naturally be the heir to the throne. There can still be no doubt that had Prince Sher Singh been the true son of Ranjít Singh, known as such by the people, he would have succeeded to the throne without opposition.

*The case of Mai Sadda Kour, which is exceptional.*

(b.) Mai Sadda Kour was the widow of Sirdár Gúrbuksh Singh Kanheya, who died in the lifetime of his father Jai Singh, chief of the great confederacy which ruled the northern portion of the Bári Doáb. Her husband was killed in 1784, leaving no male issue, and his father then divided the whole estate, including the jagírs of Gúrbuksh

Singh, over which the latter never appears to have had any absolute control, by *chundaband*, or equally between the issue of wives. Mai Sadda Kour, on the death of Jai Singh in 1796, succeeded to the half of the estate, which may be assumed as her husband's share, and subsequently to almost the entire remainder of her father-in-law's property, which had been made over to his younger sons Nidhán Singh and Bhág Singh.

*The question of the nature of Mai Sadda Kour's tenure of the Kanheya estates has lately been re-opened by Sháhdeo Singh.*

The question of the nature of Mai Sadda Kour's possession of the Kanheya territory has lately assumed additional interest from a claim advanced by Sháhzádah Sháhdeo Singh, son of the late Mahárája Sher Singh of Lahore. Sadda Kour had one daughter, Mehtáb Kour, married to Mahárája Ranjít Singh, and, of this union, Sher Singh was the reputed issue. The claim of Sháhdeo Singh is to the lands held by his father, who obtained them by gift or inheritance from Mai Sadda Kour, his grand-mother, or through his mother Mehtáb Kour. But the estates could not so devolve according to Sikh law. Sadda Kour obtained them on her father-in-law's death, not by right, for her husband had died in the lifetime of his father, who had left two other sons his lawful heirs, but because she was a woman of the greatest courage and ability, and the chiefs of the Kanheya confederacy desired her for their leader, while her brothers-in-law were feeble and unable to oppose her. But Sadda Kour had no power to bequeath her estates, nor could her daughter's son inherit them from her, as there is no succession in the female line, nor could he inherit them from his mother, who was incompetent to hold them, and as a matter of fact never did hold them. The question of succession in the female line will be referred to at greater length hereafter.

(*c.*) Ráni Dya Kour and Sukhán were the widows of Sirdár Bhagwán Singh of Diálghar, who died in 1812 without issue. The estate, which was worth nearly a lakh of rupees a year, was divided equally between the widows, who held it till their death. *Diálghar.*

(*d.*) The chiefship of Ambála was one of the most important of those held by widows South of the Satlej, and was worth nearly Rs. 60,000 a year, with many subordinate vassals. Sirdár Gúrbuksh Singh died in 1783, leaving neither sons, brothers nor nephews. His widow, Dya Kour, succeeded to the estate, which she held till her death in 1823, when it lapsed to Government. *Ambála.*

*Búria.* (e.) Ráni Nand Kour, the widow of Sirdár Jaimal Singh, succeeded to the estate of her husband, who died in 1817 without male issue. Guláb Singh, a uterine brother of Jaimal Singh, was set aside in favor of the widow, though the asserted illegitimacy of his birth influenced the decision of the Government. He however succeeded eventually to a great part of his brother's possessions, and, on the death of Nand Kour in 1835, to the share held by her.

*Biláspúr.* (d.) Mai Dya Kour succeeded to the estate of her husband, Sirdár Sher Singh, on his death, without any near male relative.

*Chiloundi.* (c.) This case is precisely the same as the preceding. No male relation of Sirdár Bhagel Singh was living at the time of his death, and his two widows, Ráj Kour and Rám Kour, succeeded him.

*Thanesar.* (f.) The chiefship of Thanesar affords two precedents of a rather conflicting nature. Sirdár Bhanga Singh left a son Fatah Singh, and a widow Mai Jíah. The former succeeded his father, and died in 1819, leaving two widows, who did not directly inherit, but the estate went to Mai Jíah, who governed in the name of her deceased son, to the exclusion of her two daughters-in-law. She died in 1836, and the widows then succeeded, and on the death of the last, Chand Kour, in 1850, the territory escheated to Government.

Sirdár Bhág Singh, the brother of Bhanga Sing, left four sons, only one of whom, Báj Singh, left issue, Jamíyat Singh, who succeeded to the whole estate, both of his father and his uncles, to the exclusion of his uncles' widows.

(*g.*) The three widows of Sirdár Sadda Singh, Ráj Kour, Hukm Kour and Sukha, succeeded to the estate of their husband, who had apportioned it among them during his lifetime. His nearest male relative was a nephew, who made no claim at his uncle's death: but when Ráj Kour died in 1824, the Government allowed him to succeed to her share. *Dhanoera.*

(*h.*) Mai Dharmoh, widow of Hamír Singh of Selimpúr, succeeded her husband, who left no near male relation. *Selimpúr.*

(*i.*) Sirdárni Jousa succeeded her husband, Bhág Singh, in the chiefship, no brother or nephew of the Sirdár surviving. *Balchappar.*

*Rudhour.* (*j.*) Sirdárni Ind Kour succeeded her husband, Dulcha Singh, whose only near male relation was an illegitimate nephew, disqualified from succession.

*Mustaphabád.* (*k.*) The same was the case with Sirdárni Gowra, widow of Mehtáb Singh of Mustaphabád.

*Firozpúr.* (*l.*) Sirdár Dhanna Singh of Firozpúr died in 1819, leaving a widow, Lachman Kour, who succeeded to the estate, although the deceased chief had both brothers and nephews. One of the latter, Bhagel Singh, during her absence on pilgrimage, in 1823, seized the territory; but he was forced by the Lahore Mahárája, at the instance of the British authorities, to give it up: the Mahárája acknowledging the complete right of the widow, who held possession till her death in 1835.

*Other instances, in which the widow succeeded on failure of male issue, brothers or nephews of the husband.* 26. In addition to the cases given above, in which widows have succeeded to their husbands' estate, reference may be made to the families of Lashkar Khán, Tírah, Sháhabád, Bhoh, Babíál, and Nilwah, in all of which the widow or widows have inherited, failing sons, brothers or nephews of the deceased chief.

*Cases in which the* 27. The instances in which the widow has been passed over in favor of relations of the husband are so numerous, both among the Mánjha and Málwa Sikhs, that it is not necessary to do more than note a few of them. Supersession of the widow was the rule, and her succession the exception. *widow has been superseded by relations of the husband.*

(*a.*) Sirdár Hari Singh Bhangi was succeeded by his brother Jhandha Singh, and he again by his brother Ganda Singh, though both chiefs had left widows.

(*b.*) Sirdár Jassa Singh, Ahluwália, left a daughter and two widows, but a distant cousin inherited the estate.

(*c.*) Sirdár Mehtáb Singh Dulehwála left two widows, but his brother Guláb Singh succeeded him.

(*d.*) Sirdár Kapúr Singh Faizullahpúria, dying without male issue, was succeeded by his nephews to the exclusion of the widow.

But the majority of cases in which brothers have obtained, or appeared to obtain, preference to the widow, are those in which she has been remarrid by *chaddardálna,* her power over the property naturally ceasing, but her rights as the legal heir nevertheless being acknowledged.

*Joint succession of widows.*

28. The joint succession of widows is not, by any means, an invariable rule. Many instances can be quoted, such as Diálghar, Dhanoura, Chiloundi, Mustaphabád and Nilwal, in which the estate has been divided between the widows. In others it has gone to the elder widow alone, the younger receiving a maintenance.

*One widow has no claim to succeed to the share of another, deceased.*

But a division having taken place between the widows; on the death of one, the other has no claim to succeed to her share, which reverts to the next of kin of the husband in the male line, if any exist, or, in default, lapses to the paramount power.

*The case of the Diálghar Sirdárnis.*

The case of the Diálghar estates will illustrate this as well perhaps as any other.

Sirdár Bhagwán Singh left two widows, Dya Kour and Sukhán, but neither son, brother or nephew. The Government desired to make an arrangement by which the elder widow, Dya Kour, should retain the estate, the younger receiving an allowance therefrom. But this compromise Sukhán steadily refused, and, in 1817, the estate was divided between them. In 1828 Ráni Dya Kour died, and

Sukhán immediately claimed to succeed. Had she agreed, in 1817, to allow the estate to remain undivided, she might possibly have had some pretension to succeed, there being no near male heirs, but there was no shadow of claim as against the right of the paramount power to resume a lapsed estate held by a separated heirless widow, and the share of Dya Kour was accordingly resumed by Government.

*The case of Ganowli, in which one widow inherited from the other.*

29. One case of an entirely exceptional nature must here be referred to, in which one widow succeeded to the share of another. Sirdár Gainda Singh, of Ganowli, having no child by his wife Sukhán, contemplated a second marriage, which, coming to her knowledge, she proposed that he should marry her full sister Raisa, which he accordingly did. Gainda Singh died in 1791, and the two sisters held the estate in common till the death of Sukhán, when Raisa retained the undivided property, which consisted of four villages dependant on the Chichrowli chief.

This case stands almost alone, and the reasons for the sister succeeding the sister are quite intelligible, though the principle is not generally allowed. The only other case in point is that of

Thanesar, where, on the death of Sirdár Fatah Singh, in 1819, his mother managed the property, although there were two widows of her son living. On his death, in 1836, the widows succeeded jointly. Rattan Kour, the elder, died in 1844, and Chand Kour, the younger, then held the whole until her death. On the other hand, there are numerous instances showing that the right of one widow does not pass to another. Ráni Anskour of Pattiála received an estate of Rs. 5,00,000, which on her death was again included in the State lands, though other widows of the Mahárája survived. The case of Chiloundi is also in point. Ráj Kour and Rám Kour, the widows of Sirdár Bhagel Singh, succeeded him, and after a long quarrel, a partition of the estate was made between them, through the neighbouring chiefs. Ráj Kour died soon after, and, in 1809, Mahárája Ranjít Singh took her share as an escheat.

*The general principle as understood by the Sikhs.*

The rule of the Sikhs was that a separated portion of a domain descends to the heirs of the person last in possession; for, the moment an estate becomes separated, each portion acquires the character of a separate domain, and descends to its nearest male heir, failing whom, it lapses to the supreme power. Any other rule would manifestly be most inconvenient, especially in a State where there were many widows, as the amount of territory gradually vesting in the widow longest surviving, would probably exceed that held by the real head of the family.

*Daughters and their issue were incompetent to succeed.*

30. Daughters or their children were incompetent to succeed to an estate, even in default of sons, widow, brothers or nephews. The reason of this is that a girl is married immediately on her arriving at the age of puberty. She is then considered to have severed all connection with her father's family, and to be only allied to that of her husband, from whom alone she is able to inherit. Scarcely a single instance can be alleged throughout the whole of the Sikh States, in which the female line has succeeded to chiefships or landed property. Were such a practice to prevail, estates would pass into the possession of other families, and the claims of elder daughters and grand-children would be likely to be superseded by those of younger daughters and their offspring.

*Instances in which the claims of the daughter and her sons have been disallowed.*

*Kakrála.*

The Kakrála case has been commented on at some length, from which it appeared that on the death of Mai Bhágbari, leaving three daughters and two grandsons, these were all passed over in favor of Bhai Pertáb Singh, the elder son of Bhai Lál Singh of Kythal, a cousin of Mai Bhágbari's husband.

*Kapúrthala*

Sirdar Jassa Singh, of Kapúrthala, left a daughter, married to Sirdár Mohr Singh, of Fatahabád, who, on his father-in-law's death, without male issue, claimed the property through his wife, but the claim was disallowed and the estate went to a second cousin.

*Krora Singhia confederacy.*

A still more significant instance is that of Sirdar Shám Singh, Krora Singhia, who left only a daughter, who became the mother of Rattan Singh, of Búri. Neither she nor her son obtained the estate, which was divided among the chiefs of the Shám Singhia confederacy. Nor was this a mere exercise of superior force, but in strict accordance with the principle excluding all descendants of the female line, the confederacy representing the paramount power, to which the estate lapsed failing heirs in the male line, to be subjected to a re-division among the several chiefs.

The widows of Sirdár Bhagel Singh, of the same confederacy, obtained his territory, although a daughter, married to Sirdár Jhanda Singh, Dullehwála, was living and had male issue.

Sirdár Sadda Singh, Panjgharia, left an only daughter, married to Sodi Jai Singh, the High Priest of the Sikhs, yet, on Sadda Singh's death, his grandson, Sodi Uttam Singh, vainly endeavoured to obtain the estate. *Panjghar.*

One or two instances there may have been of a descendant on the female side becoming possessed of an estate, but this was by force, not by law. For example: Jodh Singh, grandson of Ráni Rajindar, the daughter of Sirdár Bhumia Singh, of Pattiála, usurped her possessions, and held them for some months, when he was murdered, and the rightful heir, Chúr Mal, brother of Ráni Rajindar's husband, succeeded. *No legitimate succession on the female side, though there may have been occasional usurpations.*

31. The right of adoption, so far as it might confer on the person adopted (*pálak* or *potrèla*) a claim to inherit a chiefship or estate, is not allowed, either among the Mánjha or Málwa Sikhs. The British Government, desiring to perpetuate the more important families, has granted to certain of them the right of adoption, but this is a new right not before acknowledged. But, nevertheless, instances have occurred of chiefs, without male issue, adopting heirs, who have been permitted to succeed; but these cases, like Jhanda Singh Bhangi, the *Adoption.* *Adoption is not allowed as confirming any right to succeed to a chiefship.*

adopted son of Sirdár Híra Singh, and Nár Singh, Chamyári, the adopted son of Sirdár Sáwal Singh, who, with the sanction of the *Gúrmata*, the Sikh national assembly, succeeded to all that chief's estates, belong to the early days of Sikh history, when there was no paramount power to claim the escheat.

There is, however, no instance of inheritance by the adopted son of a widow. Ráṇi Bhágbari desired to adopt, or did adopt, Amar Singh, the son of Raja Hamír Singh of Mani Majra, but her making a will also in his favor showed that she knew such adoption to be invalid, and, in the subsequent succession, both adoption and will were disregarded.

Ráni Dya Kour, of Ambála, in the same way, desired to adopt her sister's son, but this was not permitted, and Sirdárni Dya Kour, of Biláspúr, adopted in succession, or desired to adopt, Sobha Singh, the eldest son of Sirdár Jodh Singh, of Kalsia and Rája Singh, her sister's son, neither adoption, however, having any effect upon the eventual descent of the property.

Mai Lachman Kour, of Firozpúr, adopted Bishan Singh, no relation of her own or her husband's, but on her death, in 1835, the claim to inherit was refused, and the estate lapsed to Government.

That adoption was not generally permitted is abundantly proved by the numerous lapses which fell to both the British Government and to Mahárája Ranjít Singh, none of which would have taken place had the chiefs or their widows been competent to adopt.

*The opinion of Sir H. Lawrence and Captain Murray on the subject of adoption.*

32. Sir Henry Lawrence, writing, in 1844, on this subject, observes—" It will be gathered from " all I have said that I do not consider that the " rules of succession in the protected Sikh States " have hitherto been based upon the laws of Hindú " inheritance: if they had been, we could not have " inherited a single estate: for the husbands of " each of these widows permitted by us to succeed " their husbands would have adopted children, as " several chiefs and widows have endeavoured to " do, but notoriously against the practice of their " sect. The Mai of Chiloundi, the oldest in the " protected States, being so well aware of this that " last August, when I was in her neighbourhood, " she begged my interference to secure a single

"village for a lad of her adoption; and Ráni "Sukhán of Diálghar's whole thoughts are turned "to obtaining a small reversion to her brothers. "The Sirdár of Rúpar is also bent upon making "interest for the son of his daughter. All these "facts go to prove, not only that the Hindú laws of "inheritance have not been acted upon, but that "the chiefs are well aware of what has been the "practice."

In the same way, Captain Murray, writing to Sir Edward Colebrooke in 1827, on the subject of the adoption of the younger son of Sirdár Ajít Singh of Ládwa by the widow of Sirdár Dulcha Singh of Rudour, his grandmother, says—"Such "an adoption may hold good according to the "Shásters, but, in my judgment, they are more "applicable to private and personal property than "to public Sirdárís, and the general practice of the "country favors this opinion. Were the Muham-"madan and Hindú Laws of Inheritance as in-"culcated by the Sharah and Mitáksharah to be "made the rule for our guidance, very few, if any, "of the many principalities would remain entire, "and a common distribution of landed property "would become universal, to the destruction of "estates and annihilation of the chiefs."

The recognition of the adoption of her daughter's son was refused to the Sirdárni of Rúdour, and, on her death, in 1828, the estate lapsed to Government.

ILLEGITIMACY.

*An illegitimate son has no claim whatever to succeed.*

33. There have been many doubts expressed as to the extent to which illegitimacy bars succession among the Sikhs; but after a careful consideration of the customs of the principal families, it may be laid down as a general and undoubted rule that an illegitimate son has no claim whatever as against a legitimate son. He will be entitled to maintenance from the estate, but to nothing more. Nor, where no legitimate son exists, has the right of the illegitimate son been allowed; but the inheritance has passed to the widow, the brother or the nephew, or has lapsed to the paramount power, and this principle has been maintained by the British Government itself.

*The opinion of the late Viceroy in the Kapúrthalla case, on the subject of illegitimacy.*

The late Viceroy, Sir John Lawrence, writing in May 1853, on the Ahluwália case, which has lately been again before Government, took a somewhat different view of the question.

" It is asserted," he writes, " by the present " Rája that both his brothers are illegitimate; that "their mother was a mere slave girl, and that by "the Hindú law they would not inherit. These "arguments the Chief Commissioner does not con- "sider to be tenable. In a caste so low in the soci- "al scale as that of the Ahluwália family; bastardy "would never be a sufficient cause for setting "aside the rights of male children. The ceremony "of marriage among all the various races which "are to be found among the Sikh persuasion, is but "lightly regarded. The mere fact of a *chaddar-* "*dálna* (throwing a sheet) over a female is univer- "sally considered to be a complete acknowledgment "that marriage has taken place."

The fact that the marriage ceremony among the Sikhs was often of so simple a character, and so easily performed, is a strong argument against the claims of the issue of a woman with whom no such ceremony can be proved to have been performed. It has been before shown that the *chaddardálna* marriage was fully accepted by all the Mánjha and Málwa Sikhs as amply sufficient to give the woman the full status of a wife, and to legitimatize her issue, who succeed equally with the issue of the orthodox marriage; that the chief reigning families among the Sikhs to-day, are sprung from *chaddar-dálna* marriages; and that the custom has only been abandoned lately by the Phúlkián houses, for the simple reason that the Supreme Government has granted to them the right of adoption, and has enjoined the rule of primogeniture and the exclusion of females from the succession. The *karewa* marriage, which transferred the rights of the widow to the next surviving brother, has consequently become unnecessary, as the widow, in these families, has, now, no transferable right.

*Illegitimacy, however, is of different kinds, and some illegitimate children are held in more consideration than others.*

34. There are degrees even in bastardy: and an illegitimate son born of one mother might have preferential rights to a son born of another. Two cases may be quoted as examples of this: Sirdár Bhanga Singh of Thanesar left a son, Sáhib Singh, born of a slave girl, who was declared, in consequence of his illegitimacy, ineligible to succeed conjointly with his legitimate brother. He received, however, a provision of nine and a half villages, which descended to his son Bishan Singh.

Sirdár Dulcha Singh of Rudhour was succeeded by his widow, his nephew Dasundha Singh being illegitimate, the issue of a woman whose husband was living, and who had eloped or been forcibly abducted by Sirdár Prem Singh.

On the death of Ind Kour the widow, Dasundha Singh put forward his claim, alleging that he did not obtain the estate on the death of Sirdár Dulcha Singh, as widows had prior rights to uterine brothers and nephews, but his claim was altogether disallowed; and the chiefs of Pattiála, Nábha, Jhínd and Kythal, whose opinion was asked by Captain Murray, in 1827, declared that Sáhib Singh of Thanesar was of better blood than Dasundha Singh of Rudhour, as being born of a girl who was at least the property of her master, while Dasundha Singh was merely the issue of an adulterous connection.

This claim was brought forward again, in 1837, by Fatah Singh, the son of Dasundha Singh, who had died, and was again rejected as preposterous. The opinion of the chiefs was again asked, and they were unanimous in condemning it; Pattiála alone, for interested reasons of its own, favoring Fatah Singh's claims. Even the aged widow of Sirdár Bhagel Singh, who might be supposed to desire the estate to remain in the family, wrote to Sir George Clerk to say that she considered the British Government the only heir to Rudhour and to the estate that she herself possessed, but that, in the event of the Supreme

Government relinquishing its rights in Rudhour, she was prepared to claim it in virtue of her husband's supremacy over all the Krora Singhia misl, and that, on her demise, should the Supreme Government still renounce its right to Rudhour and Chiloundi, she knew no heirs but the Bráhmans of Hardwár, on whom, in such a contingency, she begged that the estates might be allowed to devolve.

*The distinction which exists between legitimate and illegitimate concubinage.*

35. Again, the son of a girl who had come as a virgin to the chief's family, as an attendant on his first wife, is considered as of higher position and as entitled to a larger maintenance than one born of an ordinary slave girl, or of a widow taken into the *zanána* after the death of her first husband. This distinction between legitimate and illegitimate concubinage is perfectly well understood, and a similar practice prevails among the ruling Rájpút houses, where the sons of women who have come as virgins, attendants on a bride, into the chief's house, have succeeded to the throne, and have in any case been treated with the highest consideration.

*The case of Baidwán, and the claim of Basáwa Singh.*

36. An interesting case with reference to the question of legitimacy is that of Baidwán, decided

by the Government of India in March 1828. Sirdár Jassa Singh was one of three brothers, who had divided the patrimony between them. He died, leaving a widow, Sáhib Kour, and a concubine, Khem Kour, by whom he had a son, whose claim to inherit was at once advanced. The mother, Khem Kour, did not pretend to have been married to the chief, though she was of respectable birth. She had been first married north of the Satlej, and on her husband's death had lived for 15 years with her parents. Here Jassa Singh saw her, and, as she was a near relation of his wife, took her to his home and had by her a son, Bassáwa Singh.

On the death of Jassa Singh, in 1827, the succession of this child was permitted by the Political Agent. The brothers, however, opposed it, and after enquiries, which satisfied the Agent of Bassáwa Singh's illegitimacy, he recommended that he should be set aside, an allowance of Rs. 1,000 being assigned to him and his mother. But they would not accept this arrangement, and petitioned the Supreme Government, who instituted enquiries, and till the year 1835 the case remained under investigation, when it was finally compromised by the parties themselves. Of the illegitimacy of the child there was no doubt, and he was properly set aside. No marriage had ever taken place with the mother on the part of Jassa Singh, and this she had herself acknowledged. But on this occasion was raised the question whether a man could legally be married by the *karewa* ceremony, to a more distant relation than his brother's widow, and the chiefs were asked their opinion by direction of the Agent Governor General ( 7th February 1833 ).

This question again involved that of the legality among Sikhs of the re-marriage of widows. *The legality of the re-marriage of widows.*

The difference which exists between the *karewa* marriage with a brother's widow, and the same ceremony, or, more strictly speaking, *chaddardálna*, with any other woman, has been already explained ( para. 17 ).

The re-marriage of widows is common among the Sikhs, not alone with a brother's widow, but generally, on the death of her husband, a Sikh widow, whose ideas of freedom are very different from those of her Hindú countrywomen, marries again, the man of her choice, and her right to do this, if there be no brother of her late husband to claim her, is universally admitted. Sikh widows marry sometimes even a third husband, this marriage being known as *threwa*. Notwithstanding this liberty allowed to Sikh women, the practice of "*Sati*" or widow-burning, was prevalent both in the Panjáb proper and in the Cis-Satlej States till 1846, the last instance being the widow of Sirdár Shám Singh Attáriwala, who burnt herself, with her husband's clothes, the day after the battle of Sobraon.

*Sati was a common practice.*

*Illegitimate children have never inherited except in the early Sikh days, and when no legitimate claimant existed.*

37. Illegitimate children have occasionally inherited, such as Jodh Singh Kalsia, Dewá Singh and Charrat Singh of Rúpar, Búdh Singh Bulíki, and Guláb Singh of Sounti, but these instances occurred in the early days of Sikh ascendancy, and where no opposing claims of widows or brothers existed to such succession; and it may be generally affirmed that, during the last fifty or sixty years, no acknowledged illegitimate issue has been permitted to succeed to an estate, even where no legitimate male issue, brothers, nephews, or widows existed, nor, before that time, conjointly with or to the prejudice of the legitimate heirs.

*Transfer of estates by will.*

38. The custom of making a testamentary disposition of property prevails among the Sikhs,

to a limited extent; but the power of the testator is strictly limited, and must not be exercised contrary to the acknowledged rules of succession. For example, a testator could not bequeath his estate to a brother, when he had sons living: but he might leave all his property to his younger son, with a bare maintenance to the elder, provided that the custom of primogeniture had not been adopted in his family, nor an invariable rule of equal division. Should the father have disowned his son he may leave the estate to his grandson, but having these, or one of these, living, he cannot bequeath the estates to any one else. In the Cis-Satlej States wills have been generally executed with the endeavour to strengthen an illegal or extravagant claim, and they have, in most cases, been successfully disputed, but the power to dispose of landed property by will, within certain limits, has never been denied.

*A widow has, in no case, the power to execute a will, or to dispose of real property.*

39. A widow in possession of a chiefship has no power to bequeath it by will. Several times the attempt has been made, but in no case with success, and her power, indeed, only extends over personal property, which, in her lifetime, she may give to her daughter. The right of the widow to succeed,

failing male issue, does not confer upon her any absolute proprietary right, and she is considered merely as holding the estate in trust for others, with no right to dispose of more than the income. The Rája of Mani Majra, it is true, 'in 1818, declared that a widow had, both by the Shástra and Veda, the full right to will away her husband's territory and chiefship, but he only made this assertion because his own son was then hoping to succeed through the will of a widow, and the assertion was palpably false, as testamentary dispositions of property are unknown to Hindú Law, and even had a widow such power by the Shástras, she certainly had not by Sikh custom.

*Will cases. That of Rája Bhág Singh of Jhínd in 1813.*

40. Several cases of considerable interest connected with wills have occurred since the British connection with the Panjáb. First in order of time, is that of Rája Bhág Singh of Jhínd, who died in June 1813, leaving three sons, Fatah Singh, Partáb Singh and Mehtáb Singh. A year before his death he had deposited with Sir D. Ochterlony, the Agent of the Governor General, his will, by which he left to his elder son Fatah Singh, only the *iláquas* of Sangrúr and Bassian, and a request to the British Government that he might enjoy the jagírs he held from it for life. To Partáb Singh, the second

son, he left the fort and districts of Jhínd and Ludhiána, and declared him the successor to the throne. To the youngest son he left the *iláquas* of Burdawáli and Jandáli.

When the Rája first made known the provisions of this document to Sir D. Ochterlony, that officer tried to urge the claims of the eldest son, and observed that the right of primogeniture was much regarded by the English Government, but the Rája replied that the father had the right of nominating his own successor and bequeathing his lands as he pleased, and that he himself had been the second son preferred by his father. This assertion, which was also inserted in the body of the will, apparently to prove the custom of his family, did not express the whole truth. Rája Gajpat Singh, of Jhínd, who died in 1789, had three sons, of whom Bhág Singh was certainly the second. But Mehr Singh, the eldest son, died before his father, in 1781, leaving a son Harí Singh, who was sixteen years old when Bhág Singh succeeded, and who was the rightful heir had the rule of primogeniture been strictly enforced, for, although a widow, whose husband dies in the lifetime of his father has no claim, the right of a son is not invalidated by the death of his father before obtaining the chiefship. This point does not appear to have been thoroughly known when the case was submitted to the Government, and it is impossible to say whether it would have had any influence on the ultimate decision.

The Rája does not appear to have had any cause of complaint against the eldest son, and the disposition he made was only owing to Partáb Singh being the greater favorite, the son of the wife to whom he was most attached, although she had died many years before, when Partáb Singh was a mere infant.

It must be remarked that there was no doubt about the validity of the will. It was made when the Rája was in perfect health, and of sound mind, and after the subject had been deliberately discussed with the Agent of the Governor General.

*The Government refuse to sanction the will made by the Rája, and declare that in the State of Jhínd primogeniture is to be followed.*

The Government of India, to whom the will was submitted, when the death of the Rája appeared imminent, refused to sanction the disposition made by him. As this was the first decision in the Sikh States regarding the right of primogeniture, and as it asserted this rule for the chiefship of

Jhínd, while it was not till 1837 that Pattiála, Nábha, and Kythal were authoritatively subjected to it, a quotation from the decision (Secretary to Government to Colonel Ochterlony, 15th May 1813) will be of interest.

"The Governor General in Council possesses "no information which affords a ground of belief "that the laws or usages of the Sikhs generally or "the custom of Bhág Singh's family in particular, "leave to the chief the choice of a successor to the "exclusion of the eldest son. Admitting the fact "alleged by Bhág Singh, which, however, appears "from your despatch to be disputed, namely, that "he himself succeeded in preference to his brother, "it cannot be inferred from that fact that such was "the prevailing custom of the family.*

"Whatever doubt the Governor General in "Council might entertain with regard to the justice "or propriety of opposing the will of Bhág Singh, "if there were good reason to suppose that it was "warranted by the laws or usages of his tribe and

* It must however, be remembered that Bhág Singh was the first instance of a succession to the Jhínd chiefship, which had been founded by his father Gagpat Singh, so that his own case was the only possible precedent. The father of Gajpat Singh was a simple landowner, Sukhchen by name. Any authority which could be derived from his example is in favor of division among the sons, for he founded two villages, Báláuwali and Sukchen, the former of which he gave to his eldest son Alam Singh, and the latter to his second son Gajpat Singh.

" family, His Lordship in Council can have no " hesitation, under the contrary impression which " exists in his mind, in refusing to afford the coun- " tenance of the British Government to an arrange- " ment, which is, in His Lordship's estimation, no " less unjust in principle than likely to be perni- " cious in its effects. You are authorized therefore " to declare to the parties concerned, and to the " surviving friends of the family, after the death of " Bhág Singh, that the succession of Koer Partáb " Singh cannot be recognized by the British Go- " vernment. You are authorized moreover to em- " ploy the influence of the name and authority of " Government in support of the claims of the elder " son to the Ráj and to the possessions generally " of Bhág Singh, or rather to that superior portion " of them, which by the terms of the will has " together with the Ráj been bequeathed to the " second son, signifying, at the same time, that care " will be taken to secure to Partáb Singh a suita- " ble position, as well as to see the bequest to the " youngest son duly carried into effect."

This decision of Government, which, as paramount, had full right to modify the terms of the will, was probably the best possible under the circumstances, though Prince Partáb Singh took up arms to dispute it, and much disorder in the State was the result; but it cannot be said that it was in strict accordance with the customs of the Jhínd family, which had only lately acquired the chiefship; and the only existing precedents of which pointed rather in the other direction.

41. The next case of importance is that of the will of the celebrated Sirdár Jodh Singh of Kalsia, who was killed at Multán, in 1818. *The will case of Sirdár Jodh Singh of Kalsia.*

Some years before his death Jodh Singh had made a partition of his property, making over one-third to his eldest son Sobah Singh, another third to his second son Harí Singh, and retaining the remainder himself, with four forts, and authority over all the *jagírdárs, pattídárs* and other adherents of the State.

Harí Singh died soon after his father, leaving a son, Dewá Singh, about three years of age, and who naturally succeeded to his father's share.

The will only concerned the portion of the territory retained by Jodh Singh himself, and gave to Sobah Singh one-half of it, with the lands and forts called the *Sirdári* share, and authority over all the *pattidárs* and other adherents. To Mai

Jíah, the mother of the second son, Harí Singh, deceased, was allotted the remaining half for life, to revert to her grandson, Dewá Singh, at her death. The will was opposed by Mai Jíah, and by Dewá Singh. The former claimed the whole of the reserved share of her husband, on the ground that the sons had portions allotted to them by their father, and that she, as his only surviving widow, was entitled to all her husband retained for himself. She objected to the validity of the will, from its not having been signed or witnessed by any neighbouring chiefs, but only by Sobah Singh's own officials. The genuineness of the will was, however, allowed, and the only points necessary to notice, are the justice of its provisions according to Sikh law.

*The mother had no right to succeed.*

Mai Jíah's claim was worthless, as, a son and grandson living, she could not claim as a widow, but only as a mother, and in the division of possessions the mother is entitled to nothing whatever, but bare maintenance; and the will gave to her far more than she had any warrant to expect.

*The Sirdári share allowed to the eldest son, who also had authority over all the dependants of the family.*

With regard to the *Sirdári* share being allotted to Sobah Singh, who thus obtained a larger portion than his nephew, Dewá Singh, who only was to receive the reversion of his grandmother's share, it has been stated, in para. 16, that although the division between brothers was nominally equal, yet that the elder generally received a somewhat larger share, known as '*Sirdári*,' as being the head and representative of the family. The elder son, moreover, had control over all the *pattidárs* or retainers: as in the case of Guláb Singh Shahíd, who obtained authority over all the *pattidárs* of his father and younger brother Mehtáb Sing. The Sháhabád family was almost the only one, in which the *pattidárs* were under the joint control of all the sons. The *jagírdárs*, in the same way, were at the mercy of the chiefs, to expel or retain in their holdings.

The claim of Dewá Singh, the nephew, was only made at the instance of his mother, who was a sister of the Rája of Pattiála, and was for equal rights over the *jagírdárs* and *pattidárs*, and the half of all property left by Sirdár Jodh Singh independent of the estates to which, by Sikh law, all the sons had an equal right.

The Government, in October 1820, confirmed the will, giving to Sobah Singh the half of the reserved estate with the forts, and the *Sirdári* share, including the horses, elephants and guns which accompany it. But the will was modified as regarded the lands in *jagír*, which, being considered the same as those in actual possession, were divided equally between Sobah Singh and his nephew Dewá Singh. The provisions of the will regarding Mai Jíah, were maintained in their integrity.

42. It will thus appear that the decision of Government in this case was not founded on the same principle as in that of Jhínd, where the right of primogeniture was affirmed and the claim of the younger son refused. In the case of Kalsia, a large and important State, equal division between brothers was assumed to be the general Sikh rule, with a somewhat larger share to the elder as the head of the family. The third illustration will show a decision by which the elder son received a share considerably larger than his younger brothers, who nevertheless obtained so much as to make the arrangement a real partition of the State in their favor.

*The Kapúrthalla will case.*

43. Rája Nihál Singh, Ahluwália, of Kapúrthalla, died in September 1852, leaving three sons, Randhír Singh, the eldest, by his first wife, and Bikráma Singh and Suchet Singh by his second.

He had been very desirous of leaving his whole territory and the succession to the Ráj to his youngest son, but from this he had been dissuaded by the British authorities. He executed a will, by which he left the larger portion of his territory to his eldest son, and to each of the two younger an estate of one lakh of rupees, unencumbered with charges for *jagírs*, pensions or Government *nazrána*, all of which were to be paid from the Rája's share.

The revenues of the State were, at this time, Rs, 5,77,763, and the *nazrána* payable to Government was Rs. 138,000, while *jagírs* chargeable on the revenues were Rs. 51,372. The division thus nominally gave two lakhs a year to the elder son, and one lakh to each of the younger, but the numerous claims of pensioners, and of relatives for maintenance, all of which were borne by the Rája, reduced his share of clear income to little more than a lakh.

The will was submitted to the Board of Administration, who approved of it, and forwarded it for the sanction of the Governor General. Before this sanction was received the Rája died, and the Board requested that no action might be taken till their further report, on the receipt of which the Governor General confirmed the will in every particular, and declared that the shares of the two younger sons should be divided off whenever they so desired.

From that time the Rája of Kapúrthalla has endeavoured to get the will set aside, but the Viceroy, in February, 1868, re-affirmed the decision of his predecessor in 1853, and directed that effect should be given to it without delay. Against this final decision the Rája appealed to the Home Government, who, maintaining the validity of the will, have directed that the younger brothers' shares should be held on a life tenure, and have given the elder brother full administrative jurisdiction over the whole territory.

It would be inconvenient to discuss the merits of a claim so recently under adjudication, and into the determination of which many political considerations have, of necessity, entered. The points, however, having direct relation to Sikh law, urged by the Rája, may be noted. These were that the rule of primogeniture must be followed in the descent of chiefships: the elder son obtaining the territory and the Ráj; and the younger sons only maintenance: and secondly, that the younger sons of Rája Nihál Singh were illegitimate, and incompetent to succeed.

*The will of Sirdár Ranjít Singh of Baidwán.*

44. The last case to be noticed is that of Sirdár Ranjít Singh of Baidwán. This chief died in 1822, leaving three sons, Jassa Singh, Bhúp Singh, and Arbel Singh, who divided the patrimony among them. Not till May 1828, did the widow come forward with a will, purporting to have been executed by her husband, disinheriting his three sons and leaving the whole of his possessions to her. Her explanation of her long silence was that she had, ever since her husband's death, been kept in strict restraint, and the reason for her husband's disposition of his property was to be found in the fact that his sons had treated him with great cruelty, and had kept him in confinement till released by an order from Captain Birch, the Political Agent.

This will was set aside, its genuineness being exceedingly doubtful; and however reprehensible may have been the conduct of the Sirdár's sons, he had no power to disinherit them altogether.

*The right of widows to dispose of estate by will.*

45. No single case can be discovered in which widows have been allowed to bequeath

*The case of Ráni Bhágbari of Kakrála.* landed property by will. There are, nevertheless, a few instances on record of such attempts being made, as was the case with Ráni Bhágbari of Kakrála, widow of Bhai Karam Singh. She, having no near relatives of her husband living, bequeathed her territory to Sirdárs Goverdhan Singh and Amar Singh, sons of Rája Hamír Singh of Mani Májra by her youngest daughter, Mai Chand Kour.

The claim was preferred in June, 1818, but was disallowed, no precedent, establishing the validity of a will made by a widow having been found.

*The will of Ráni Ind Kour of Rudhour.* In the same way, Ráni Ind Kour, of Rudhour, executed a will bequeathing the estate, which she had inherited on the death of her husband Sirdár Dulcha Singh, to a son of the Sirdár of Ládwa. A claim founded on this deed was brought forward after the death of Ráni Ind Kour, but was rejected, although there appears to have been no doubt of its genuineness.

*Collateral succession and escheat.* 47. The rights of collaterals, under Sikh law, are not easy to define, for the reason that no fixed rule has been followed, in cases of collateral succession, by the Government, whose policy has sometimes been to allow and sometimes to deny the right, as the escheat of an estate appeared to them desirable or inconvenient. At the same time, it is not difficult to determine the principle, disregarded in certain cases, but still not denied, that no collateral could, of right, succeed to a chiefship. This general principle must be held subject to some modification; but that this was the central idea of the Sikh law of inheritance there can be no doubt.

*The right of collaterals to succeed is not admitted in the Sikh States.*

Chiefships were considered altogether different from private real property, in the mode of their descent. Among the Málwa Sikhs, a private estate, on default of lineal heirs, would revert to a collateral descendant, notwithstanding his separation and enjoyment of an independent portion of the property of the common ancestor. But chiefships were governed by a different rule, which recognized the right of a paramount State to succeed in certain cases as the ultimate heir. In the Jhínd succession case, where Sirdár Sarúp Singh, of Bazídpúr, claimed the estate of his great-grandfather Rája Gajpat Singh, he desired the territory to be considered as private property and subject to the ordinary rules of inheritance. But the estates of Gajpat Singh were held entirely on a different tenure. He was a *taalúkdár* of the Dehli

Emperor, giving him service, and paying revenue, and he was, on one occasion, carried to Dehli and kept there a prisoner for three years on account of arrears of revenue, by Bakshi Najíf Beg; as, for similar reasons, the Pattiála chief was captured and taken to Sirhind in the reign of Muhammad Sháh, and as Bhai Lál Singh, the chief of Kythal, was carried to Dehli and there tortured.

*The Sikh chiefs when they came under British protection were in the same position with regard to it as they had before occupied with regard to the Emperors of Dehli.*

48. The Málwa Sikhs, when, after a period of comparative independence, they placed themselves under the protection of the British Government, assumed to it the same position that they had held to the Emperor of Delhi. Their privileges were no greater than before; their competency to alienate estates was no further extended; their relations to the paramount power were no less clearly defined. If the right of claiming escheats, on failure of lineal heirs, was denied to the British Government, its assumption of the protectorate of the States was altogether a mistake. This protectorate was a source of constant anxiety, trouble and expense. The chiefs, the moment that they had escaped the danger of absorption by the Lahore Mahárája, turned their hands against each other, and their perpetual disputes and intrigues, gave rise to innumerable political complications

and necessitated the maintenance of a large force on the north-west frontier. Was it through motives of humanity and benevolence alone that the Government assumed this inconvenient and odious charge, to save from the rapacity of Ranjít Singh the chiefs who had sought its protection? No such an assertion has ever seriously been made. The Government of Lahore, rapacious and unscrupulous as it might be, was a thousand times better, in every way, than that of the Cis-Satlej chiefs, which was infamous beyond all traditions of misgovernment, and, if the interests of the people had been concerned, the British Government would have allowed Ranjít Singh to complete his conquests to the south of the Satlej, and destroy for ever the power of the tyrannical chieftains, who were only a curse to the country.

But the Government does not appear to have been influenced by considerations such as these. It accepted the protectorate of the Cis-Satlej States on certain well-understood conditions, the principal of which was undoubtedly that its position towards the States should be the same as that formerly held by the Muhammadan Emperors; and that to it, as paramount, all estates should lapse, on failure of direct heirs. If the general right of collateral succession had been allowed, neither Búria, Firozpúr, Biláspúr, Kythal, Mustaphbád, Ambála, Thanesar, Rudhour, Diálghar, nor a single other estate, would ever have lapsed to Government.

*The Lahore Government did not recognize the rights of collaterals, but on failure of lineal heirs the estate lapsed.*

49. The only Sikh State which bore to its dependants the same relation that the Cis-Satlej chiefs bore to the British Government, was that of Lahore. There is no doubt as to the procedure followed by Ranjít Singh. The right of collateral succession was altogether denied; and, on failure of lineal male heirs, an estate lapsed, unless the Maháraja re-granted it, as was generally the case, to some near relation, on payment of a large *nazrána* or fine. This *nazrána*, paid by a collateral succeeding, was a complete admission that such succession was by favor of the supreme power, not by right; yet the Sikhs of the Mánjha had a far stronger title to secure, by collateral succession, the permanency of their chiefships than those of the Málwa, for they were true conquerors, possessing the lands they had themselves won, and independent of the Dehli Government, to which the Málwa Sikhs had been subordinate, and by connection with which their privileges and rights had been reduced or modified.

*The custom of karewa marriage shows that the right of collaterals must have been denied.*

50. That collateral succession was theoretically denied among the Sikhs is proved by the custom of *karewa* marriage, of which it is impossible to understand the origin if collateral succession was permissible. Its only object undoubtedly was to give the brother a right which he would otherwise not have possessed. The only cases of collateral succession in the principal Phúlkián families, previous to 1836, were those of Rája Amar Singh of Pattiála, Rája Hamír Singh of Nábha, and Rája Gajpat Singh of Jhínd, and in each of these the brother succeeded through a *karewa* marriage with the widow. It is not asserted that these chiefs would not have succeeded had no such marriage taken place, for the right of the widow was constantly disregarded; but it may be certainly maintained that their legal succession to the estate was through the widow, and that, without a union with her, the estate would not legally have passed collaterally.

*The succession of brothers and their children was however so common that collateral right may be so far admitted.*

51. The cases in which brothers and brothers' children have succeeded to estates, independently of the right conferred through a *karewa* marriage, are, however, numerous; and it may perhaps be conceded that, as far as these two classes of rela-

tions are concerned, collateral succession was not uncommon. In paras 19, 20, 21 and 27, instances have been given of the succession of brothers or nephews to the prejudice of the widow; generally, it is true, by violence or fraud, but still to be accepted as precedents of more or less value. But with brothers and nephews the right of collateral succession must be held to cease, and it was only, under exceptional circumstances, and for reasons of State policy, that the Government allowed the claim of cousins or of distant kindred. The decision in the Kakrála case, in 1819, which has already been discussed at some length, and by which the estate passed to a second cousin, was avowedly founded on no precedent.

*The case of the disputed succession to the Jhínd State in 1835.*

52. The most interesting case which has occurred, since the English connection with the Sikh States, with reference to the question of collateral succession, is that of the chiefship of Jhínd, and which, although not decided in accordance with either Sikh law or the precedents which the Government had itself created, is yet of so important a character that some detailed notice of it cannot with propriety be omitted here.

The following genealogical tree will explain the

position :—

- **TILOKHA.**
  - Gúrditta, from whom has descended the Nábha family.
  - Sukhchen.
    - Alam Singh.
    - Rája Gajpat Singh, died in 1789.
      - Mehr Singh, died 1781.
        - Hari Singh, died 1791.
      - Rája Bhág Singh, died 1813.
        - Fatah Singh, died in 1821.
          - Rája Sangat Singh, died in 1834.
        - Partáb Singh, died in 1815.
        - Mehtáb Singh, died in 1814.
      - Bhúp Singh, the founder of the Badruka family.
        - Karam Singh, died in 1817.
          - Sarúp Singh.
        - Basáwa Singh, died in 1830.
          - Sukhá Singh.
          - Bhagwán Singh
    - Buláki Singh.

Rája Sangat Singh of Jhínd died in 1834, without issue, his nearest male relations being his second cousins, Sarúp Singh, Sukhán Singh and Bhagwán Singh. Sáhib Kour, the elder widow of Rája Fatah Singh and mother of Rája Sangat Singh, assumed charge of the State, for, during the minority of her son she had acted as regent, and for some months no direct claims were advanced to the vacant throne. The chiefs of Pattiála and Kythal then determined on pressing the claim of the nearest collateral heir, Sirdár Sarúp Singh, the chief of Bazídpúr, having discovered that they could obtain more from him than from Ráni Sáhib Kour and the other widows. The Rája of Nábha then advanced his claim as a collateral; Sirdár Sukhá Singh on the same ground; the widows of the late Rája; the widows of his father; and, lastly, Ráni Bhágbari, the widow of Prince Partáb Singh. With reference to several of these claims a few words only are required.

(*a.*) The Rája of Nábha claimed, at any rate to share, as being a descendant from the same ancestor as the Rája of Jhínd. But his claim was disallowed, on the ground that the chiefship of Jhínd had been founded by Rája Gajpat Singh subsequently to his severance from the Nábha branch.

(*b.*) The widows of the late Rája had, undoubtedly, according to Sikh law, a valid claim to inherit. But the eldest, Subha Kour, was only twenty-three years of age, and the two younger were mere children. It was felt that it would be dangerous in the extreme to trust so important a charge as the principality of Jhínd into such feeble hands, and the claims of Subha Kour to inherit exclusively, and of the younger widows for a partition, were alike disallowed.

(*c.*) Ráni Sáhib Kour, the elder widow of Rája Fatah Singh, claimed, in the same way, to succeed, while the second widow demanded partition. The elder Ráni might, with justice, have claimed the regency had a minor succeeded, but to inherit herself was preposterous, as the mother has no right in any case of succession.

(*d.*) Mai Bhágbari, the widow of Prince Partáb Singh, claimed, as the elder widow of Rája Bhág Singh's favorite son; but Partáb Singh never had assumed the chiefship himself, and no rights could be acquired through him.

*The claimants reduced to the chiefs of Bazídpúr and Badruka.*

53. The dispute then, as to the succession, supposing the Government declined to treat Jhínd as an escheat, lay between Sarúp Singh of Bazídpúr, and Sukh Singh of Badrúka, and of these the title of Sarúp Singh, as the son of the elder of two brothers, appeared preferable. But several con-

siderations of more or less weight were urged by Sirdár Sukhá Singh. In the first place, he insisted that the custom in the Jhínd family, as instituted by Rája Bhág Singh was the succession of the second son in preference to the elder. It is quite true that Bhág Singh endeavoured to place his second son on the throne; not wishing to establish any rule for the future guidance of the family, but simply because Partáb Singh was his favorite; yet sanction to this arrangement was altogether refused by the British Government, after whose authoritative ruling, in 1813, primogeniture must be held to prevail in the Jhínd family. Sirdár Sukhán Singh, moreover, forgot that his own argument would exclude him in favor of his younger brother.

*Sarúp Singh alleged to have been disinherited by his father. The legal effect of such action.*

The second and stronger objection to Sarúp Singh was that his father, Karam Singh, had been disowned and disinherited, and was therefore incompetent to succeed. It is not possible to discover whether Karam Singh was absolutely disinherited by his father, but the probabilities are much in favor of this having taken place. He was a man of bad character, and quarrelled with Sirdár Bhúp Singh, whom he refused to obey, and moreover took forcible possession of Bazídpúr, entirely separating himself from his own family, who held no further communication with him, and, on the occasion of Bhúp Singh's death, his younger son, Bassáwa Singh, performed the funeral obsequies alone. The Rájas allied to the family, who, it is alleged, had entirely agreed in the propriety of disinheriting the elder son, nevertheless decreed that each son should obtain a moiety of the patrimony, though, in reality, the younger son Bassáwa Singh obtained two-thirds and the elder Karam Singh one-third only. Karam Singh tried hard to obtain the family estate of Badruka, but in vain, and, at that time, 1816, the Rája of Pattiála addressed Sir David Ochterlony to the effect "that "Karam Singh had for eight years previously, "during his father's lifetime, deserted the paternal "abode, and resided separately at Bazídpúr, but "that, had he remained with his father during the "lifetime of the latter, then, on his father's "decease, he would not have been excluded."

Although by Hindú Law a son who had been expelled by his father and who had not taken a share in the performance of his funeral obsequies would have no title to inherit, yet, among the Sikhs, and in a chiefship of which primogeniture was the accepted rule, it does not appear that the father has the power to disinherit the elder son. If the custom were equal or arbitrary division among the sons, his power to disinherit one would probably not be questioned. Sirdár Sarúp Singh was, at any rate, disinherited or not, held to have a better title than his cousin Sukhá Singh, and the question then arose, to what portion of the Jhínd territory was he entitled to succeed, his power, as a collateral, to succeed at all, being granted.

*The composition of the Jhínd territory.*

54. The Jhínd State consisted of three distinct portions. Rája Gajpat Singh, the founder of the family, had himself acquired Karnál, Jhínd and other territory subject to the Emperors of Dehli. His son Bhág Singh acquired Bassain, Ludhiána, and other less well known tracts, with the aid or by the direct grant of the Rája of Lahore, previous to the treaty of 1809. Lastly, there were the estates of Halwára, Talwandi, Morindah, with a moiety of Gyáspúrah and Múdki, granted to Bhág Singh by the Rája of Lahore, subsequent to the treaty of 1809.

*To what amount of territory could the claimant be considered entitled.*

Of this territory Sirdár Sarúp Singh could only be considered entitled to that portion which was in the actual possession of Rája Gajpat Singh, through whom he claimed; the remainder lapsing to the British Government as paramount, with the exception of the Lahore grants, subsequent to 1809, which justly reverted, on failure of heirs, to the original donor.

55. This was the decision of the Governor General, in his despatch, No. 103 of the 11th February 1837 :— *The orders of Government, allowing him only so much as had been in possession of his common ancestor.*

" It has been resolved by the Right Honorable " the Governor General in Council to recognize " the right of Sirdár Sarúp Singh to succeed to the " possessions of his great-grandfather, Gajpat Singh, " and accordingly to relinquish to Sarúp Singh " the tracts of country generally, which belonged " to his ancestor Gajpat Singh, through whom he " derives his titles, with the exception to be here- " after noticed.

(3). " The possessions which were granted " by Mahárája Ranjít Singh, subsequently to the " treaty of 1809, are to be made over to the " officers of His Highness.

(4). " Ludhiána and all the other possessions " acquired by the descendants of Gajpat Singh, " subsequently to the death of that chief and before " the year 1809, have lapsed to the British " Government."

In conclusion, there was laid down an authoritative rule for future guidance in questions of succession to the four greater principalties:—

"Where authorities are so conflicting, and "the practice so unsettled, as they appear to be "in the tract of country referred to, His Lordship "in Council is of opinion that it is proper and "expedient that some general principles should, "where practicable, be established by the British "Government, and every consideration of usage, "justice and policy, seems to require that, as regards "the four principal chiefships of Pattiála, Jhínd, Ky-"thal and Nábha, the rule ought to be that the estate "should devolve entire to the nearest male heir, "according to the Hindú Law, and to the exclusion "of females. With regard to all the other Sikh es-"tates, the custom of the family must be ascertained "in each instance by the best evidence procur-"able.

"Applying the above principle to the case of "Jhínd, Sarúp Singh would unquestionably appear "to have the best claim, but he can have no right to "succeed to more than was possessed by his great-"grandfather Gajpat Singh, from whom he derives "his title."

56. The Court of Directors, in a despatch dated the 8th of November 1837, was disposed to adopt a still more lenient view of Sarúp Singh's title, and considered that any lands, not received by grant from Ranjít Singh, or the British Government or its predecessors, might justly be treated as private property, in which case Sarúp Singh would be the legitimate heir. This ruling was not of any great importance, but the principle it involved might be fairly questioned, since the chiefship of a State like Jhínd was, as regarded the paramount power, one and indivisible, and any lands acquired otherwise than by grant from the Supreme Government were nevertheless held, under its protection and authority, on a tenure precisely similar to those received by a direct grant.

*This ruling as to the rights of collaterals was somewhat modified by the Court of Directors.*

57. The case of Jhínd is no more than an instance of a State which might justly have been considered to have escheated to the Supreme Government, being allowed to revert, by favor and not by right, to the nearest collateral. That this rule has not been the one always or often followed by Government is abundantly clear, and although the subject of the rights of collaterals and the principles which govern escheats is so intricate and vast, that its merest outlines can be given in a

treatise like the present, it is necessary to notice briefly three other cases, occurring shortly before or shortly after that of Jhínd, in two of which the claims of collaterals were practically denied, in accordance with what appears to be the undoubted Sikh custom, and the equally undoubted rights of the Supreme Government; and in the other, where the claim of the widows as against Government was refused, although it had before been allowed in the same family.

*The case of Thanesar, in which the claim of the widows was denied, the estate lapsing to Government.*

58. The chiefship of Thanesar, which is the last referred to, may be considered first. Sirdárs Bhanga Singh and Bhág Singh conquered Thanesar from the Bhais of Kythal, in the latter part of the eighteenth century, and divided the territory between them, Bhanga Singh taking three-fifths and Bhág Singh two-fifths. The latter Sirdár left four sons, three of whom died childless, and the whole estate came into possession of Jamíyat Singh, the son of the youngest, who died in 1832, when the territory lapsed to Government.

There was, it is true, in this instance, no near collateral, who could have succeeded, except Bishan Singh, descended from an illegitimate son of Bhanga Singh, and consequently incompetent to inherit. The only legitimate son of Bhanga

Singh had died, without issue, and his share of the territory was in the hands of his widows. Yet the widows of Jamíyat Singh were not permitted to succeed. The letter of Mr. Secretary Swinton, of the 1st of October, 1832, explains the reasons for assuming the management of the estate :—

" It appeared to the Vice President in Council " to be clear that the chiefship did not belong to " another party, and that, under an equal division " of the territory among the four claimants, the " chiefship would be abolished, or rather that the " British Government would have to exercise the " duties of chief, without any resource to meet the " necessary expenses on that account."

The Vice President in Council therefore agreed that " the widows of the late chief should be allowed " a provision out of the revenues of the estate, equal " to the highest amount received by any of the " widows of former chiefs."

*The difference between this case and that of Jhínd.*

The chiefship of Jhínd was allowed to revert to a collateral, as if it had been private property, the widows being set aside on political grounds alone. But the territory left by Jamíyat Singh was small, and no great inconvenience could have arisen from its division among his widows.

With far greater justice than Jhínd might they have urged that the estate should devolve according to the ordinary rules of succession. The Jhínd chief had been a dependant of the Muhammádan Emperors of Delhi, paying tribute, and punished when he failed to do so. The chiefs of Thanesar, on the contrary, had conquered their territory from its old possessors, by their own swords, they had been independent from the first, and had never paid tribute to any power, until brought under the protection of the British Government. Nor had the widows of Jamíyat Singh to go far for precedents in support of their claim, when the widows of Sirdár Fatah Singh, Rattan Kour and Chand Kour, were then in possession of Bhanga Singh's share of this very estate.

*The escheat of Búria was of somewhat the same character.*

The escheat of Búria, or rather of that portion of it held by Sirdár Megh Singh, was somewhat similar to that of Thanesar. The chief died in 1835, when Sir George Clerk assumed charge of the estate for Government, although the deceased had left two widows. It is, however, true that Megh Singh had repudiated these ladies, whose characters were indifferent, and desired them to be excluded, not only from inheritance but even from maintenance.

*The lapse of Firozpúr to Government, who refused to allow the claim of collaterals to succeed.*

59. The case of Firozpúr will show that the British Government had no intention of maintaining, under all circumstances, the rights of collatérals.

Sirdar Gúrbaksh Singh, d. 1823.

- Dúna Singh.
  - Bhagel Singh, d. 1826.
  - Chanda Singh.
  - Jhanda Singh.
- Dhana Singh. d. 1818.
- Súrmukh Singh.
- Jai Singh.

Sirdár Gúrbaksh Singh was a follower and relation of Sirdar Gujar Singh, the leader of the great Bhangi confederacy, and conquered Firozpúr, town and territory, in 1772. By his three wives he had four sons, among whom, in the year 1794, he divided his territory. To Dúna Singh, the eldest, he assigned Sitáraghar and Badian, north of the Satlej; to Dhana Singh, the second, he gave the fort and territory of Firozpúr, to the south of the Satlej; to the third and fourth sons, Súrmukh Singh and Jai Singh, he allotted Sanjára and Naggar respectively, north of the Satlej; and retained Singhpúrah for himself. In 1818, Sirdár Dhana Singh died, without issue, and was succeeded by his widow Mai Luchman Kour in the possession of Firozpúr. In 1820 she proceeded on a pilgrimage to Gya; and Bhagel Singh, son of Dúna Singh, and nephew of her husband, took advantage of her absence to seize the territory. The agent of the Ráni appealed to Captain Ross, the Deputy Superintendent of Sikh affairs, who addressed the Lahore Court, when the Maharája, recalling Bhagel Singh, who was in his service, and who, in all probability, had made the raid with his consent if not assistance, declared that the right of the widow was indefeasible, as holding a share separated off for her husband in the lifetime of his father.

*The death of Ráni Lachman Kour, when Firozpur escheated, though nephews of the late chief were alive.*

60. Ráni Lachman Kour died in 1835, still in possession of Firozpúr, although both Ranjít Singh and the British Government, knowing its value as a military position, had tried to effect an exchange with the widow for other territory elsewhere. On her death the estate lapsed to Government.

Sirdar Gúrbuksh Singh had died, in 1823, and Bhagel Singh, the nephew, who took forcible possession of Firozpúr in 1826, was also dead. But his two brothers, Chanda Singh and Jhanda Singh, were still alive, as were the sons of Súrmukh Singh, a vassal of the Attáriwála chief, and the former, in July 1838, preferred their claim to inherit, to Sir George Clerk at the Amballa Agency. The question was referred for the determination of the Supreme Government, and was decided against the claimants. The letter of the Secretary to Government, of the 24th November 1838, was to the following effect :—

"The claimants are descendants of Dúna Singh, "to whom his father Gúrbuksh Singh assigned "possessions on the northern bank of the Satlej, "making over to his second son Dhana Singh, "Firozpúr and its lands as a separate allotment, and "a distinct tenure, thus constituting, according to "the Hindu Law and Sikh customs, two separate "and distinct families.

"On Dhana Singh's death, this separated por-"tion of Gúrbaksh Singh's acquisitions came into "possession of his wife Lachman Kour, and, on her "decease, lapsed as one of the Protected States to "the British Government.

"The nephews of Dhana Singh have clearly "no right to the separated portion of their uncle, "and their claim to it is disallowed accordingly."

*The decision of Government in this case would also have applied to the State of Jhínd.*

61. This decision was undoubtedly in accordance with the acknowledged law regulating succession to Sikh States; but its arguments would have applied with equal if not greater force to the case of Jhínd, which had been decided in the

preceding year. There, the principality had been made over to a second cousin, a member of a family altogether separate and distinct from that of Jhínd. Sirdár Bhúp Singh, the grandfather of the claimant of the Jhínd principality, had founded the Badrúka State, altogether separate from that of Jhínd, and the succession to which was governed by different rules; and not only this, but Karam Singh, the father of the claimant, had again separated himself, absolutely and entirely, from the Badrúka State, and had founded the independent chiefship of Bazídpúr, so that on the death of his father the Badrúka property devolved on the second son. If Sirdár Sarúp Singh, of Bazídpúr, a second cousin of Rája Sangat Singh, was held to have any title to Jhínd, it does not appear on what grounds the claim of the nephews of the chief of Firozpúr was disallowed. The only satisfactory explanation appears to be that, in both cases, the territory was a legitimate escheat, but the British Government did not wish to assume the direct management of the principality of Jhínd, while Firozpúr was a position which they had long desired to obtain as a military post.

*The lapse of the Kythal State, on the death of Bhai Udai Singh.*

62. In the year 1843, the State of Kythal lapsed to Government, on the death of Bhai Udai

Singh. The principle which governed this escheat was mainly that laid down, in 1837, with reference to the succession of Jhínd, and there would be no necessity to allude to it here, had not the practice of the Bhaikián family, and the precedent of the Kakrála case, seemed to give some claim to a collateral to succeed to all the possessions of heirless members of the family.

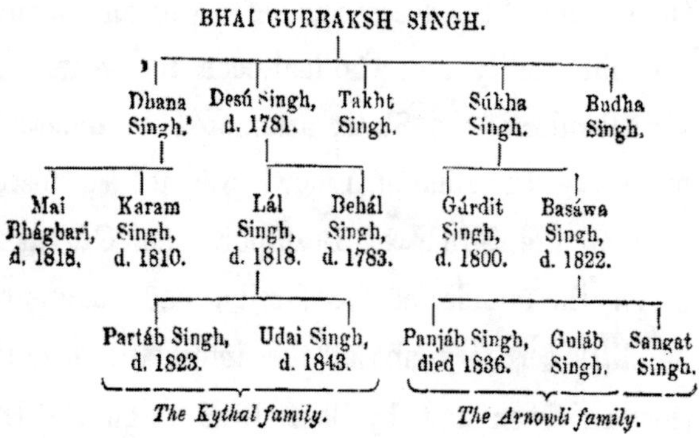


*The decision in this case followed the ruling laid down by Government in the case of Jhínd.*

63. On the death of Bhai Udai Singh, in 1843, the only claimants of the estate were Bhais Guláb Singh and Sangat Singh, the chiefs of Arnowli, who, for three generations, had been separate from the Kythal branch of the family. The two widows of Udai Singh were, under the order of Government of 1837, excluding females from succession to the Kythal State, incompetent to inherit.

The principle laid down in the Jhínd case was followed in that of Kythal; the claim of the Arnowli branch to succeed to the acquisitions of the common ancestor, Bhai Gúrbaksh Singh, was admitted, and all subsequent acquisitions were declared to have lapsed to the British Government.

This decision was received with great dissatisfaction by the Cis-Satlej Rájas, and, in Kythal itself, the mother of the deceased chief, a woman of considerable ability, and who had been for years the virtual ruler of the State, attempted to oppose it by force. The Bhai of Arnowli was not so fortunate as the Sirdár of Bazídpúr: for Gúrbaksh Singh, the founder of the family, had conquered but little territory, and all the important acquisitions had been made by Bhais Desú Singh and Lál Singh, and consequently lapsed to Government.

Bhai Guláb Singh, supported by the Mahárája of Pattiála and the Rájas of Nábha and Jhínd, insisted on his right to the whole territory owned by Bhai Udai Singh.

*The practice of the Bhaikián seemed to favour the rights of collaterals.*

The practice which had prevailed in the family, and which, in truth, was but violence opposed to law, seemed to give some colour to this claim. Bhai Gúrbaksh Singh divided his territory equally among his sons, who each added to his share of the patrimony, but, in 1808, it was found that Bhai Lál Singh, whom Sir David Ochterlony, (letter 15th November 1811) believed to have received only one hundred villages from his father, (and this was a most exaggerated estimate), was master of the whole territory, with the exception of a small portion held by his cousins Karam Singh and Basáwa Singh. He had either succeeded to or taken possession of almost all that his uncles Takht Singh and Búdha Singh and his cousin Gúrdit Singh had owned. Nor was the claim of the Arnowli branch weakened by the fact that although the British Government had, in 1811, admitted the claim of the widow of Bhai Karam Singh to her husband's patrimony to be stronger than that of the cousin Bhai Lál Singh, yet, that on her death, in 1818, it had allowed its own indefeasible right to claim the escheat, to be set aside in favour of Bhai Partáb Singh, a distant collateral.

The claim of Bhai Guláb Singh of Arnowli to the Kythal principality was justly disallowed, but what he received of the possessions of his ancestor Bhai Gúrbaksh Singh, he would certainly not have obtained under any Hindu Government, nor under the Sikh Government of Lahore, to whom, under similar circumstances, the whole estate, ancestral with that recently acquired, would undoubtedly have lapsed.

CONCLUSION.

*The changes which have, since the annexation of the Panjáb, been introduced by the British Government, briefly noticed.*

64. The chief features of the Sikh law of succession to chiefships, as it existed at the time of the first Sikh war, before the British Government, by the compulsion of circumstances and by considerations of policy, had assumed the direct management of the Panjáb proper, and had completely revised the terms of its connection with the Cis-Satlej States, have now been considered. The scope of this treatise, which is rather historical than legal, is too limited to include the law and the precedents which have grown up since 1849, sometimes in opposition to the practice which formerly prevailed, but more often in modification of it. It will not, however, be useless to notice, with the utmost briefness, the more notable changes which have been introduced by the direct action of the British Government.

*Primogeniture.*

65. So early as 1813, on the occasion of the death of Rája Bhág Singh of Jhínd, the Government had declared the rule of primogeniture to be in force in that family. In 1837, when it was again necessary for the Government of India to determine

the succession to the principality of Jhínd, it was ruled that primogeniture was to be held to prevail in the four States of Pattiála, Nábha, Jhínd and Kythàl, and that, on failure of sons, the nearest male heir should succeed, to the exclusion of females; a collateral, however, possessing a right to no more than had been held by the common ancestor from whom he derived his claim. The Court of Directors, in the same year, extended the title of the collateral to all other possessions which had not been acquired by grant from the British Government or its predecessors.

*Rules laid down by Government in 1851 regarding collateral succession to pattidári shares in the Cis-Satlej States.*

66. In 1851, on the motion of the Board of Administration, the Supreme Government sanctioned the following rules regarding collateral succession to *pattidári* shares in the Cis-Satlej States, including almost all the minor chiefships:—

"Your Board have requested that a distinct "rule should be laid down by the Government, "respecting the succession to such shares on which "conflicting decisions have hitherto been given by "the several officers in charge from time to time.

"After careful consideration of the whole "question, aided by the documents which have "recently been submitted, His Lordship has come

" to the conclusion that the following rules should " be finally adopted for the regulation of succession " to horsemen's shares above mentioned:—

" (1.) That no widow shall succeed.

" (2.) That no descendant in the female line " shall inherit.

" (3.) That, on failure of a direct male heir, " a collateral male heir may succeed if the common " ancestor of the deceased and collateral claimant " was in possession of the share at, or since, the " period, 1808-9, when our connection with the Cis- " Satlej territory first commenced.

" III. On a former occasion, the Governor " General expressed an opinion that each question " of succession should be governed by a reference " to the status of 1808-9. It was intended that " the right of possession should be recognized as " belonging to those who were in possession of the " property in 1808-9, and that the right of succes- " sion to such property should be conceded not " only to such male heirs, but also to the collateral " male heirs of those who were so in possession in " or since that year. The rule is liberal. No " Native State would concede so great an indulgence " as to allow succession to collaterals at all; while

" to give effect to that rule from the period of our " first connection with the country, forty years ago, " of course increases the indulgence by extending " its advantages to a greater number.

" IV. The limitation of the rule to the date " 1808-9 is just and reasonable, for, if the right of " succession to any share were granted to the colla- " teral heirs of the person who originally obtained " it, at however remote a period, great difficulties " would arise in the determination of such rights. " Your Board state, in reply to a question put to " you, that you consider it practicable to ascertain " correctly the possessions of 1808-9.

" V. This rule clearly laid down will govern " the majority of cases which occur, and His " Lordship does not see any necessity for establish- " ing an absolute rule in the case of large estates. " Each case may, without any difficulty, and with " great advantage, be determined upon its own " merits as it arises. His Lordship would, how- " ever, remark generally that consideration of the " custom of families should have a preponderating " influence in the decision of such cases.

" VI. Though the rule now laid down may " be at variance with the course which has been " actually taken in many cases, the Governor

"General would, by no means, disturb the decisions "which have been given. All parties who have "received possession from a British officer should "retain it for their own lives, except females, who "should receive pensions instead."

*Supplementary rules sanctioned by Government.*

67. It soon appeared that these rules would, in certain cases, be difficult to apply, and, in January 1852, the following supplementary rules were proposed and approved:—

(1.) That a specific order of Government, even though opposed to the principles and rules now proposed, shall avail, in favor of the party concerned and his lineal male heirs.

(2.) That the mere fact of a female having been in possession in 1808-9 shall not avail to stop succession, or to invalidate successions that may have taken effect. This rule not to extend to females, who, since 1808-9, have succeeded to shares, unless they should have so succeeded with the knowledge and sanction, or under the orders, of the Political Agent.

(3.) That the official and recorded declaration of the Political Agent as to the person in possession in 1808-9, shall be accepted without question, and the succession continued accordingly.

(4.) That alienations by a jagírdár or pattídár, of portions of his holding, shall neither be officially recognized nor officially recorded.

(5.) That one or more sons of a common ancestor, in possession in 1808-9, being entitled to the whole share possessed by such common ancestor, shall be held, and be declared, responsible for the maintenance of widows left by deceased brothers, who, had they lived, would have shared with such son or sons.

(6.) That private exchanges of shares during times past, be recognized, provided that fraudulent intent be not established.

(7.) That parties who have had no specified possession since 1808-9, have no valid claim either to share or pension.

(8.) That the Settlement Officer, on the Civil side, shall take cognizance of claims to recovery of shares of which the claimants may have been wrongfully dispossessed, subject to the provisions of the statute of limitations.

(9.) That the enquiry shall not extend into possessions of the zaildárs or dependants of an individual Sirdár during the lifetime of such Sirdár.

(10.) That on the estate of such Sirdár lapsing, the possessions of his zaildárs shall be enquired into, ascertained and recorded, and that from and after the date of lapse of the Sirdár's estate, lapses of the zaildárs' shares and successions to the same shall follow the first and second of the rules prescribed by the orders of Government, No. 461, of 12th February 1851.

*Further orders of Government with reference to the right of widows in possession.*

68. In February 1853, the Government sanctioned more liberal pensions for widows, but ruled, with regard to male heirs who had succeeded to widows in possession in 1808-9, that they should retain such estates for their respective lives only.

In June 1853, the Supreme Government received from the Court of Directors a despatch relative to the rules sanctioned for pattídári estates, generally approving of the same, and objecting only to the admission of collateral branches to succeed, provided they were descended from the individual who was in possession in 1808-9; and to the exclusion of widows, extending even to those still in possession.

The Court sanctioned, however, the rule passed with reference to collaterals, but ruled that the widows in possession should not be disturbed, and that those who had been dispossesed should receive pensions equal to the net revenue of their estates, deducting commutation fixed for all service due from them.

New rules were accordingly framed with regard to the pensions of widows, which were approved by the Court of Directors, who directed that widows who had been in possession for less than seven years should receive pensions equal to the full value of their estates.

*The pensions of widows were to be proportionally diminished if the revenue of the resumed estate was smaller than had been estimated.*

69. Meanwhile a question had arisen as to how far a subsequent decrease in the revenue of the resumed estate should affect the pensions of *pattidári* widows, and it was ruled that the pension should be proportionately decreased, as it was granted only as an equivalent for the actual value of the estate, which was subsequently discovered to have been over-estimated.

*The right of adoption conceded to the principal chiefs.*

70. A change in the policy of Government with reference to escheats has, of late years, taken place. With a desire to see the Native States perpetuated, the Government has granted to the more important Chiefs and Rájas the right of adoption in default of male issue. Sanads of adoption were granted to the Maháraja of Pattiála, and the Rájas

of Jhínd and Nábha on the 5th of May 1860, conferring on these chiefs and their heirs for ever, whenever male issue might fail, the right of adopting a successor from among the descendants of the Phúlkián family. If, however, at any time, any one of these three chiefs should die without adopting a successor, then it would still be open to the two remaining chiefs, in concert with the Commissioner or Political Agent of the British Government, to select a successor from among the members of the Phúlkián family, but in that case, a *nazrána* or fine equal to one-third of the gross annual revenue of the State was to be paid to the British Government.

On the 5th March 1862, a Sanad of adoption was granted to Rája Ranbír Singh of Kapúrthalla, and during the same month to the Rája of Farídkot, the Sirdár of Kalsia, Rája Tej Singh, and Sirdár Shamsher Singh Sindhanwália.

*The Government desire to introduce generally the rule of primogeniture in all estates.*

71. The Panjáb Government was desirous of substituting, if possible, the law of primogeniture for the various usages which regulated hereditary succession to conquest and ordinary jagírs held in perpetuity. The Governor General (letter 12th May 1860) agreed with the Panjáb Government that primogeniture should be encouraged,

but directed that no alteration in the rule of inheritance should be made in a family unless with the consent of its head and of the chief members interested. The Panjáb Government (Circular No. 636 of 25th May 1860) directed its Commissioners to explain to the several chiefs the advantages of primogeniture in the maintenance of the power and importance of chiefships, and in cases where chiefs were willing to accept the rule as binding upon them, to draw up a formal deed, which should alone be of force to determine the legal transmission of such jagírs. The success of the Government proposal was very partial. A considerable number of chiefs and jagírdárs admitted the advantage of the rule of primogeniture, and executed deeds binding themselves to observe it, but a large number were unwilling to adopt it, principally out of consideration for their younger sons, who would be reduced to a mere maintenance, or be entirely dependent on the elder brother for support.